Do It Yourself

Unschooling Journal

Name: & Age:

Address:

Phone & Email:

Instructions

LIST or DRAW NINE THINGS

That you want to learn about:

1.
2.
3.
4.
5.
6.
7.
8.
9.

Action Steps:

1. Go to the library or bookstore.

2. Bring home a stack of at least NINE interesting books about these topics. Choose some that have diagrams, instructions and illustrations.

Supplies Needed:

You will need pencils, colored pencils, pens and markers.

Choose Nine Books To Use As School Books!

1. Draw each book cover or write down the titles on each cover below.
2. Keep your stack of books in a safe place, add new books as needed.
3. Be ready to read a few pages from your books daily.
4. You may complete 5 to 10 pages in this book each day, depending on your goals.

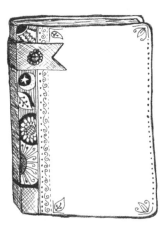 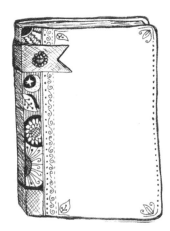 

 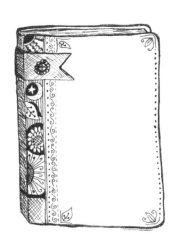 

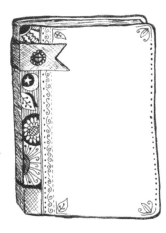 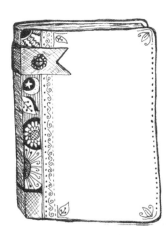 

When you choose new books, add them to the back of this Journal.

Priority and Planning

Date:_____

A Quote

_____
_____
_____
_____

To-Do List

_____
_____
_____
_____

My Plans

_____
_____
_____
_____

My Goals

_____
_____
_____

Notes:

_____
_____
_____
_____

Travel Dreams Geography

Choose any City, any State or any Country:

Where would you like to go?

How far would you travel?

What would you pack?

----

what would you see?

What would you eat?

What is the weather like?

What makes this place unique?

Share an interesting fact:

Draw something you would see in this place:

Reading Time - 1 Hour (Set a timer)

Choose Four Books - Read from each book for 15 minutes.

Copy important words or pictures from each book here:

Relax and be Creative

Practice working with your colored pencils.

Object Lesson

Look at this picture.

List four things that you understand about the object.

1._____

2._____

3._____

4._____

Just be Creative.

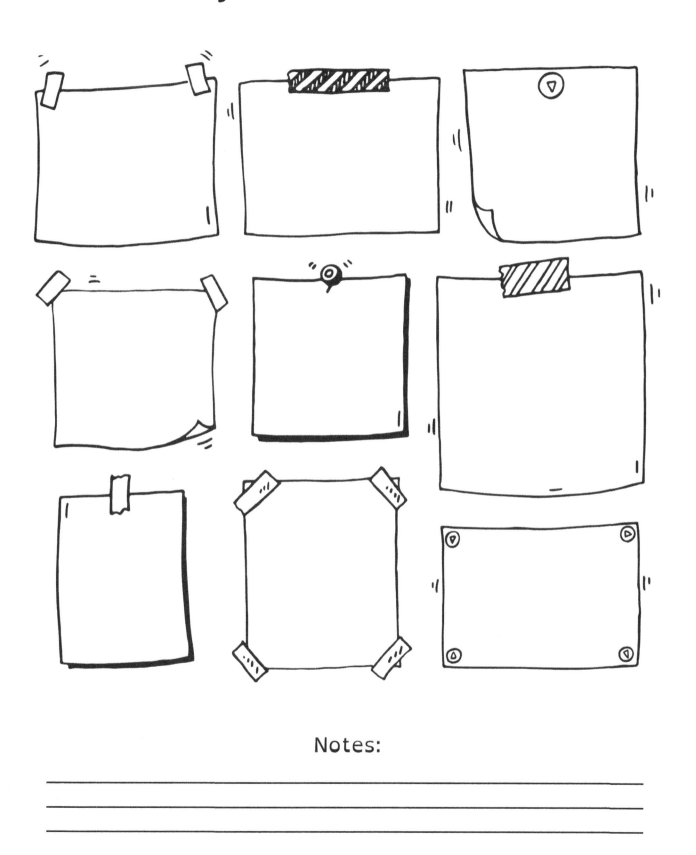

Notes:

_____

_____

_____

Spelling Time

Find 20 Words with **8** letters each.
Look around your house and in your
books for words. Write the words here:

Screen Time!

Watch a Documentary, Educational Program, Movie, or Tutorial.

Start Time: _____

Stop Time:

TITLE: _____

SUBJECT _____

LOCATION: _____

MESSAGE: _____

Rating:

AWFUL

BAD

LAME

YUCKY

OKAY

NICE

GOOD

GREAT

SUPER

Draw a Scene from the video:

Notes:

TITLE:

Use THIS PAGE for Math Practice

Or be creative and design something, like a house! You could make graphs, maps or geometric designs with this graph paper.

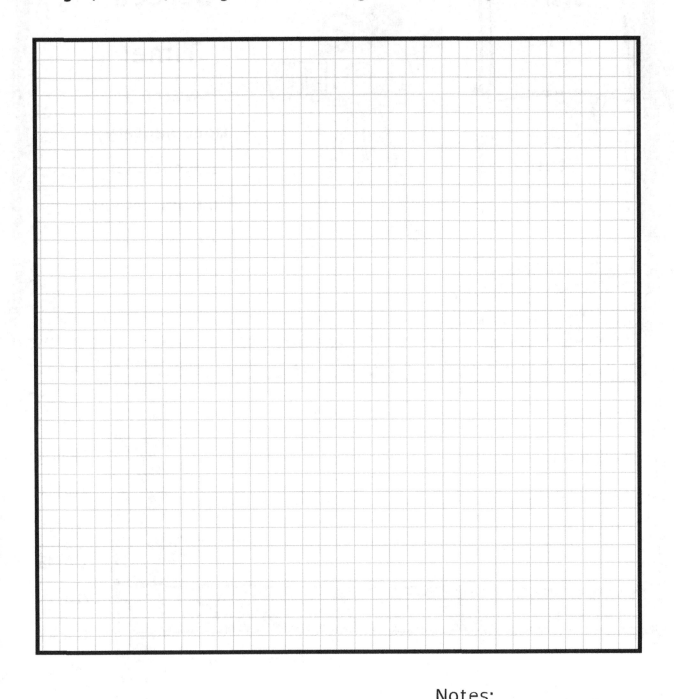

Notes:

_____

_____

_____

_____

World News Today!

Talk to your parents about current events.

Look at a newspaper, news broadcast or website.

Color the countries your learn about.

Tell the news stories with words or pictures.

Book of the Day

Choose a book from your stack that you want to focus on today.

Write and Draw to show what your are learning.

TITLE:_____

Thinking Time!

Can you complete the puzzle?

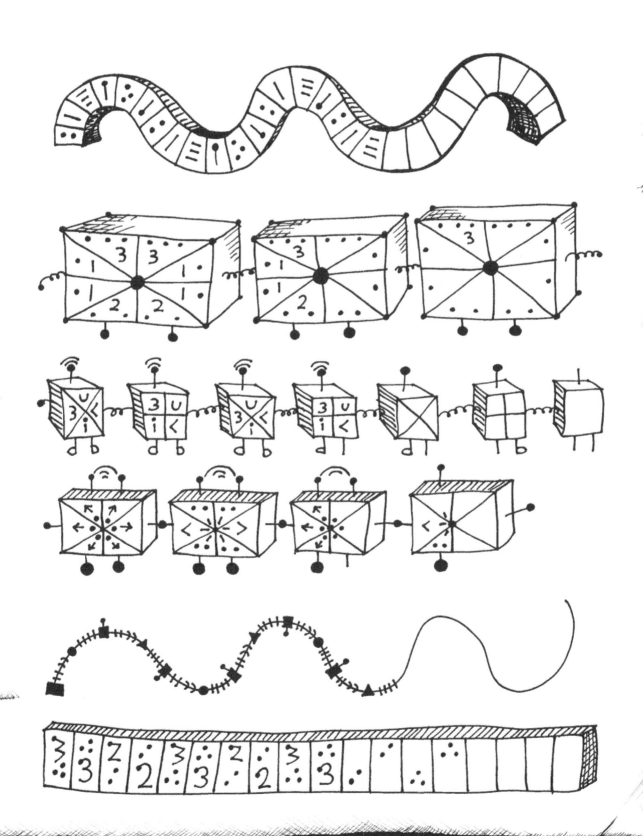

Travel Dreams Geography

Choose any City, any State or any Country:

Where would you like to go?

How far would you travel?

What would you pack?

----

what would you see?

What would you eat?

What is the weather like?

What makes this place unique?

Share an interesting fact:

Draw something you would see in this place:

Priority and Planning

Date:_____

A Quote

_____
_____
_____
_____

To-Do List

_____
_____
_____
_____
_____

My Plans

_____
_____
_____
_____

My Goals

_____
_____
_____
_____

Notes:

_____
_____
_____
_____
_____

Relax and be Creative

Practice working with your colored pencils.

Object Lesson

Look at this picture.

List four things that you understand about the object.

1. _____

2. _____

3. _____

4. _____

Just be Creative.

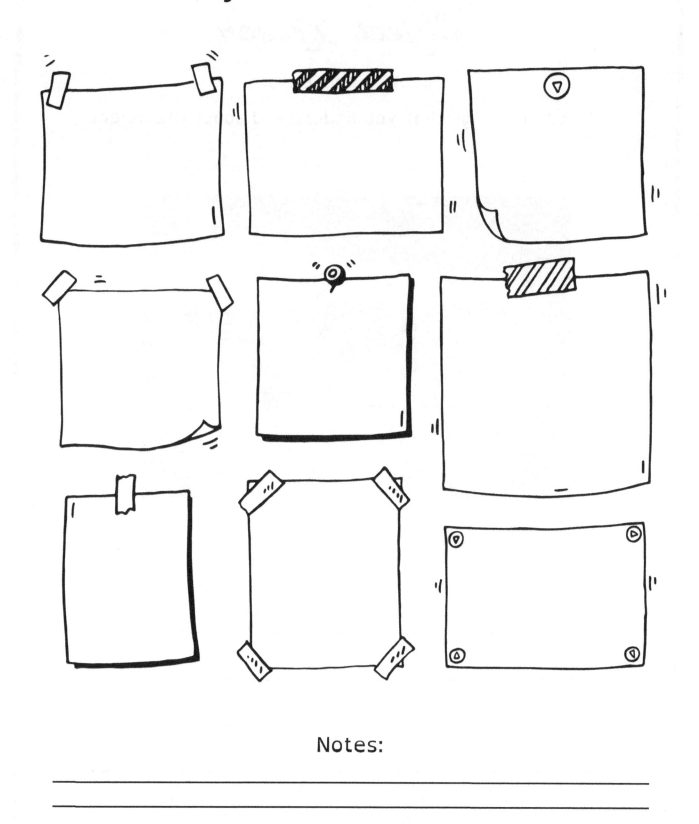

Notes:
_____
_____
_____

Nature Study

Go outside and make a realistic drawing of something you find in nature.

Reading Time - 1 Hour (Set a timer)

Choose Four Books - Read from each book for 15 minutes.

Copy important words or pictures from each book here:

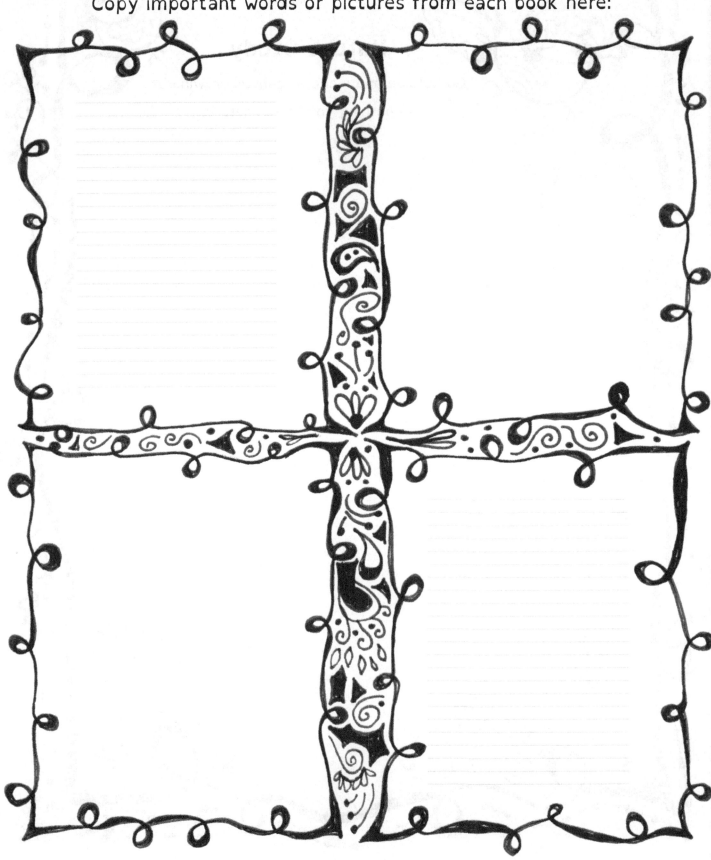

Spelling Time

Find 20 Words with **5** letters each.
Look around your house and in your
books for words. Write the words here:

_____	_____
_____	_____
_____	_____
_____	_____
_____	_____
_____	_____
_____	_____
_____	_____
_____	_____
_____	_____

Start Time:

Stop Time:

Screen Time!

Watch a Documentary, Educational Program, Movie, or Tutorial.

TITLE: _____

SUBJECT _____

LOCATION: _____

MESSAGE: _____

Rating:

AWFUL

BAD

LAME

YUCKY

OKAY

NICE

GOOD

GREAT

SUPER

Notes:

TITLE:

Draw a Scene from the video:

Use THIS PAGE for Math Practice

Or be creative and design something, like a house! You could make graphs, maps or geometric designs with this graph paper.

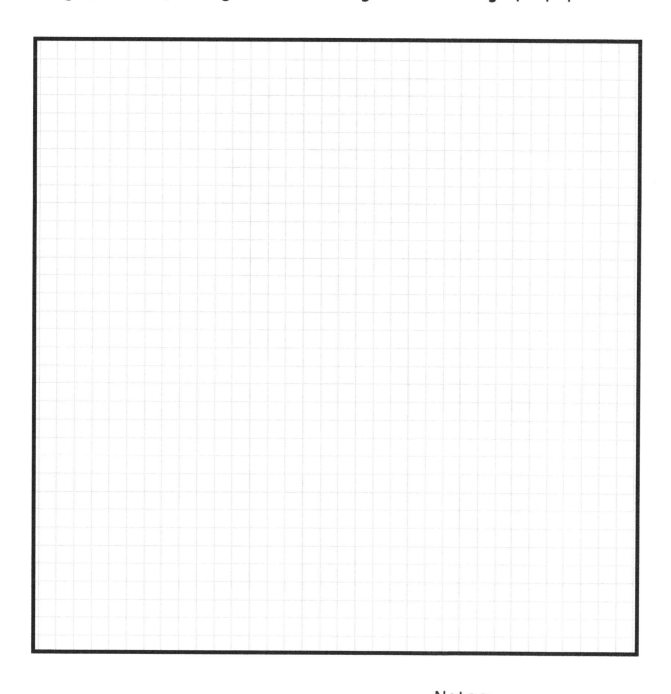

Notes:

_____

_____

_____

_____

Book of the Day

Choose a book from your stack that you want to focus on today.

Write and Draw to show what your are learning.

TITLE:_____

Thinking Time!

Can you complete the puzzle?

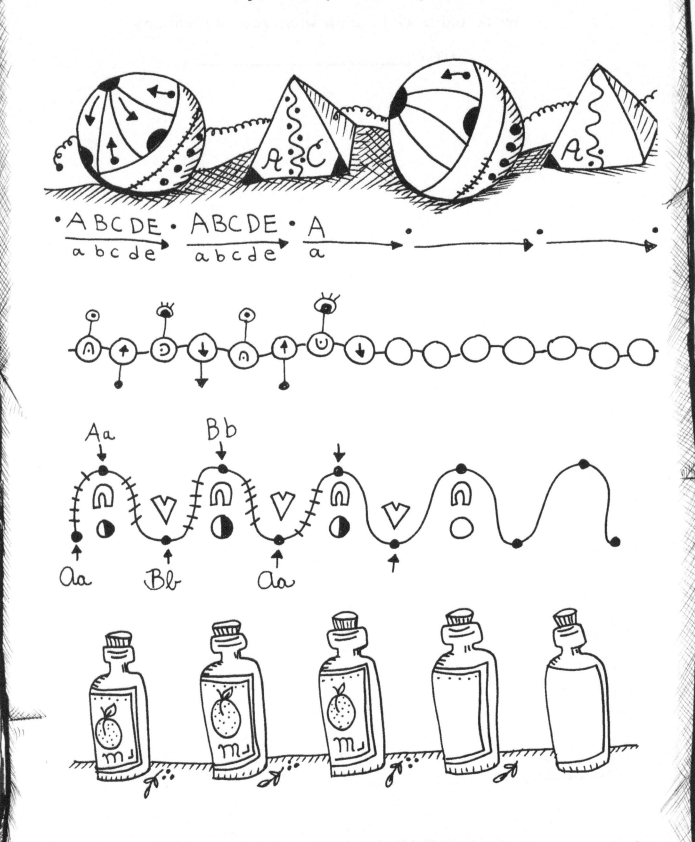

Travel Dreams Geography

Choose any City, any State or any Country:

Where would you like to go?

_____

How far would you travel?

_____

What would you pack?

_____

what would you see?

_____

What would you eat?

_____

What is the weather like?

_____

What makes this place unique?

_____

Share an interesting fact:

_____

Draw something you would see in this place:

Priority and Planning

Date:_____

A Quote

_____
_____
_____

To-Do List

_____
_____
_____

My Plans

_____
_____
_____

My Goals

_____
_____
_____

Notes:

_____
_____
_____
_____
_____

Relax and be Creative

Practice working with your colored pencils.

Object Lesson

Look at this picture.

List four things that you understand about the object.

1. _____

2. _____

3. _____

4. _____

Nature Study

Go outside and make a realistic drawing of something you find in nature.

Reading Time - 1 Hour (Set a timer)

Choose Four Books - Read from each book for 15 minutes.

Copy important words or pictures from each book here:

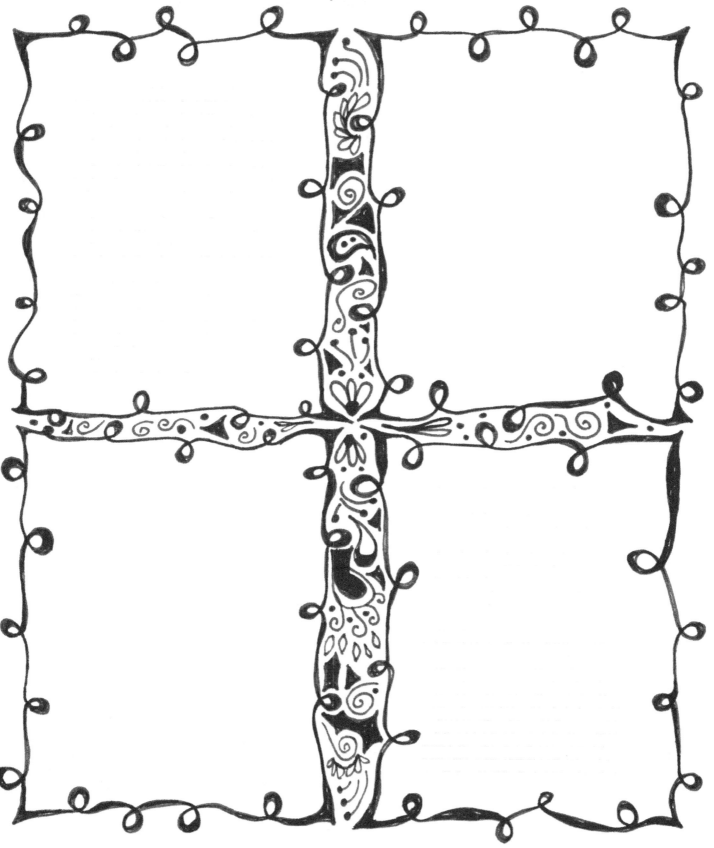

Spelling Time

Find 20 Words with 8 letters each.
Look around your house and in your
books for words. Write the words here:

Start Time:

Stop Time:

Screen Time!

Watch a Documentary, Educational Program, Movie, or Tutorial.

TITLE: _____

SUBJECT _____

LOCATION: _____

MESSAGE: _____

Rating:

AWFUL

BAD

LAME

YUCKY

OKAY

NICE

GOOD

GREAT

SUPER

Notes:

TITLE:

Draw a Scene from the video:

Use THIS PAGE for Math Practice

Or be creative and design something, like a house! You could make graphs, maps or geometric designs with this graph paper.

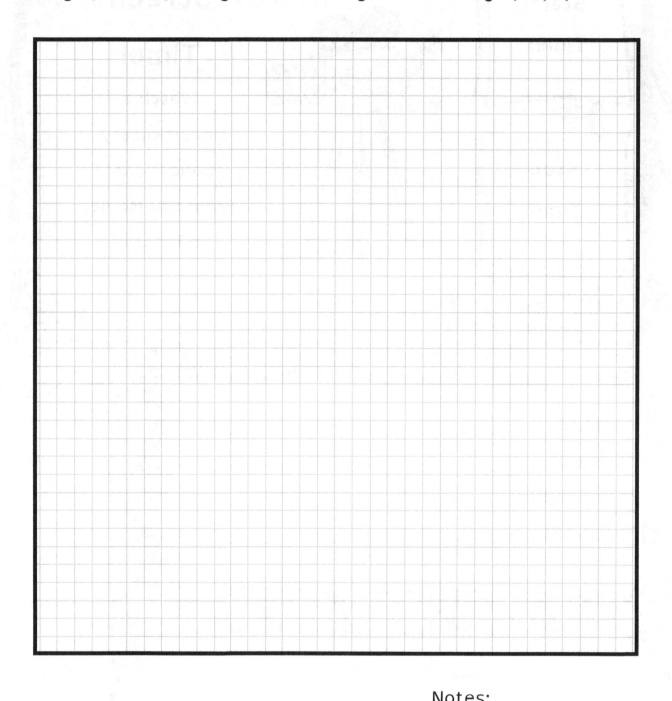

Notes:

_____

_____

_____

_____

Font Writing Practice:

ABCDEFGHIJKLMNOPQRSTUVWXYZ

abcdefghijklmnopqrstuvwxyz

ABCDEFGHIJKLMNOPQRSTUVWXYZ

ABCDEFGHIJKLMNOPQRSTUVWXYZ

Abcdefghijklmnopqrstuvwxyz

Develop Your Own Style

Book of the Day

Choose a book from your stack that you want to focus on today.

Write and Draw to show what your are learning.

TITLE:_____

Thinking Time!

Can you complete the puzzle?

Travel Dreams Geography

Choose any City, any State or any Country:

Where would you like to go?

How far would you travel?

What would you pack?

----

what would you see?

What would you eat?

What is the weather like?

What makes this place unique?

Share an interesting fact:

Draw something you would see in this place:

Priority and Planning

Date:_____

A Quote

_____
_____
_____
_____

To-Do List

_____
_____
_____
_____

My Plans

_____
_____
_____

My Goals

_____
_____
_____

Notes:

_____
_____
_____
_____
_____

Object Lesson

Look at this picture.

List four things that you understand about the object.

1._____

2._____

3._____

4._____

Just be Creative.

Notes:

_____

_____

_____

Nature Study

Go outside and make a realistic drawing of
something you find in nature.

Reading Time - 1 Hour (Set a timer)

Choose Four Books - Read from each book for 15 minutes.

Copy important words or pictures from each book here:

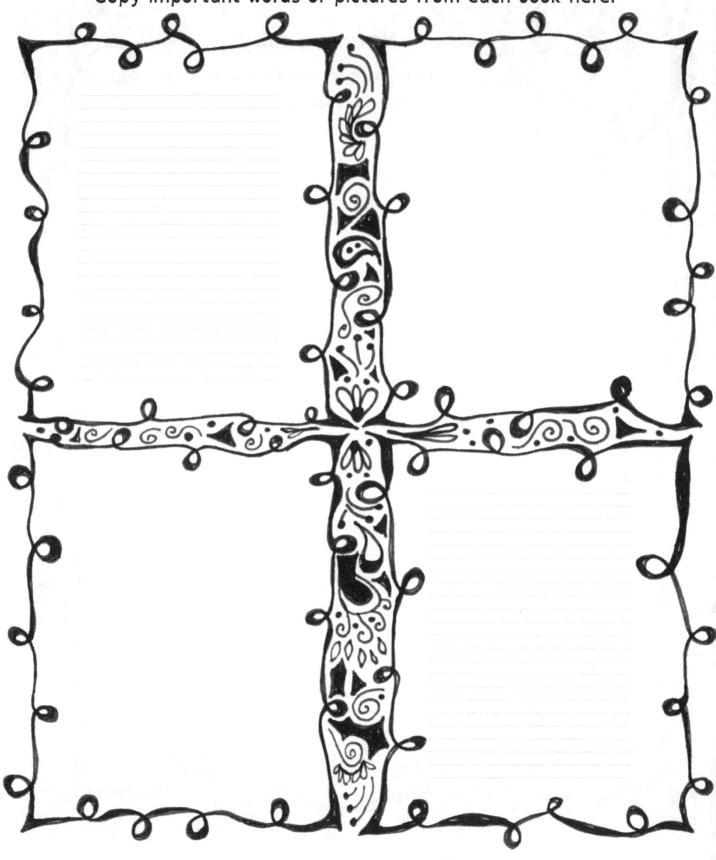

Spelling Time

Find 20 Words with 7 letters each. Look around your house and in your books for words. Write the words here:

Start Time: _____

Stop Time: _____

Screen Time!

Watch a Documentary, Educational Program, Movie, or Tutorial.

TITLE: _____

SUBJECT _____

LOCATION: _____

MESSAGE: _____

Rating:

AWFUL

BAD

LAME

YUCKY

OKAY

NICE

GOOD

GREAT

SUPER

Draw a Scene from the video:

Notes:

TITLE:

Use THIS PAGE for Math Practice

Or be creative and design something, like a house! You could make graphs, maps or geometric designs with this graph paper.

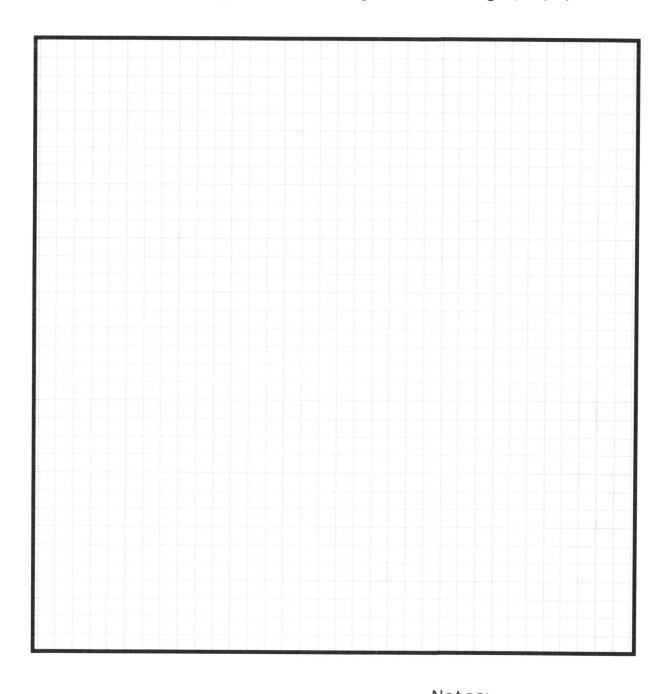

Notes:

_____

_____

_____

_____

Book of the Day

Choose a book from your stack that you want to focus on today.

Write and Draw to show what your are learning.

TITLE:_____

Thinking Time!

Can you complete the puzzle?

Travel Dreams Geography

Choose any City, any State or any Country:

Where would you like to go?

How far would you travel?

What would you pack?

----

what would you see?

What would you eat?

What is the weather like?

What makes this place unique?

Share an interesting fact:

Draw something you would see in this place:

Relax and be Creative

Practice working with your colored pencils.

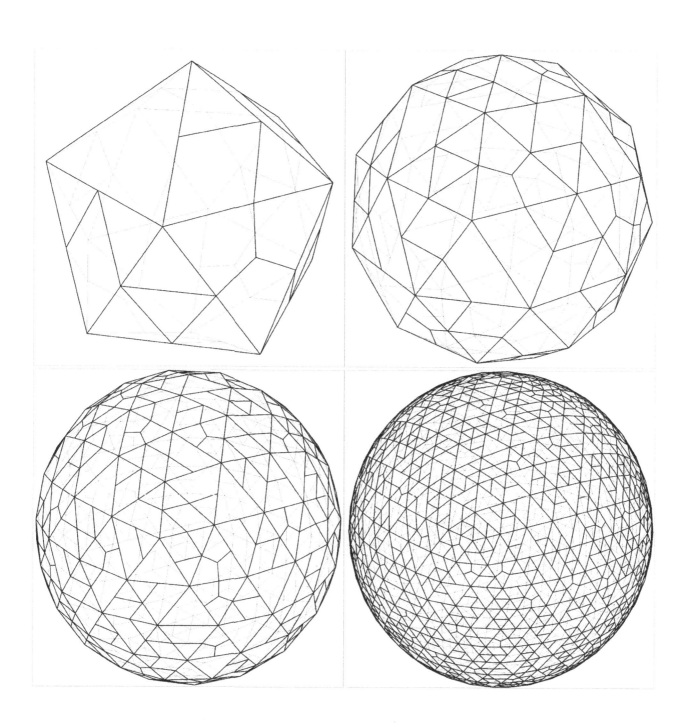

Object Lesson

Look at this picture.

List four things that you understand about the object.

1._____

2._____

3._____

4._____

Journal

A Day in My Life

Nature Study

Go outside and make a realistic drawing of something you find in nature.

Reading Time - 1 Hour (Set a timer)

Choose Four Books - Read from each book for 15 minutes.

Copy important words or pictures from each book here:

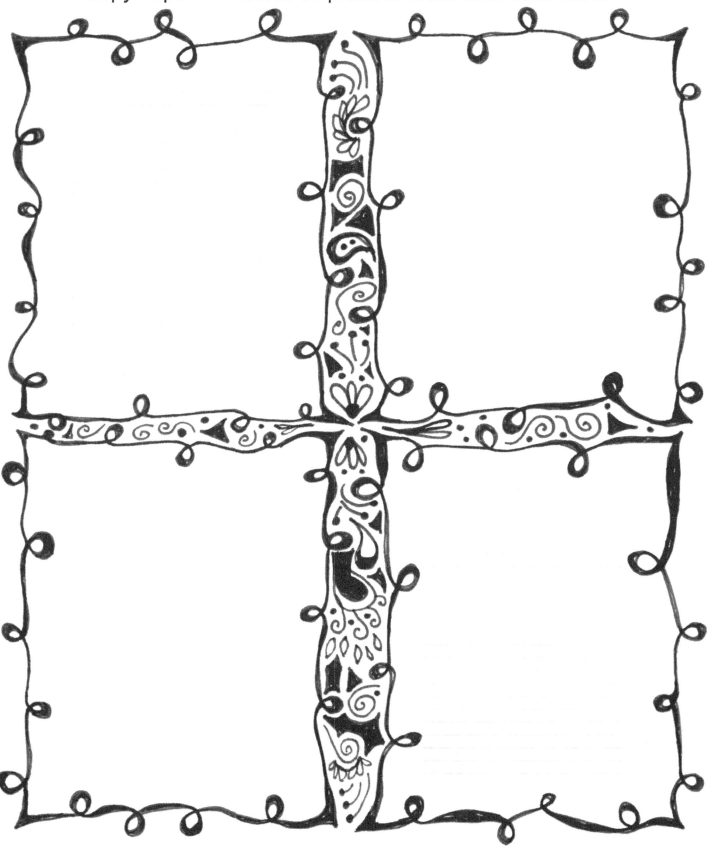

Spelling Time

Find 20 Words with **8** letters each.
Look around your house and in your
books for words. Write the words here:

_____   _____

_____   _____

_____   _____

_____   _____

_____   _____

_____   _____

_____   _____

_____   _____

_____   _____

_____   _____

Start Time:

Stop Time:

Screen Time!

Watch a Documentary, Educational Program, Movie, or Tutorial.

TITLE: _____

SUBJECT _____

LOCATION: _____

MESSAGE: _____

Rating:

AWFUL

BAD

LAME

YUCKY

OKAY

NICE

GOOD

GREAT

SUPER

Draw a Scene from the video:

Notes:

TITLE:

Use THIS PAGE for Math Practice

Or be creative and design something, like a house! You could make graphs, maps or geometric designs with this graph paper.

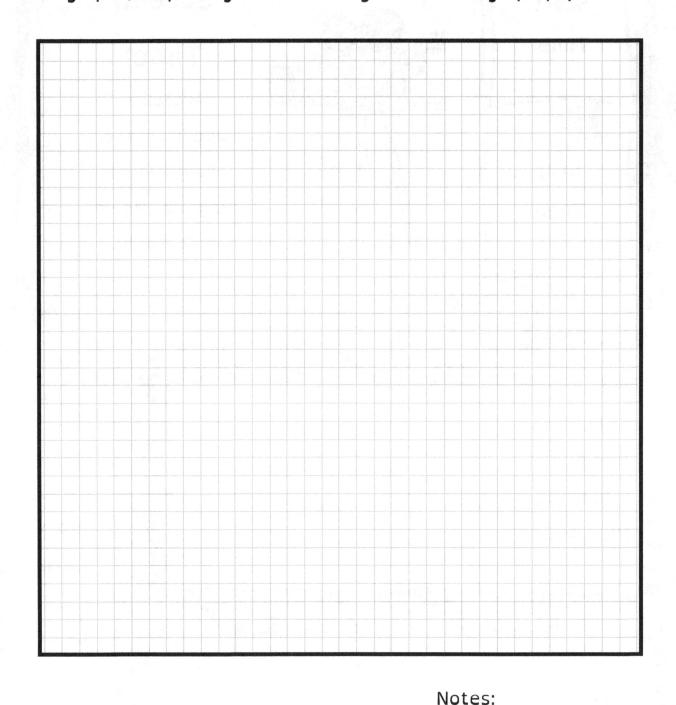

Notes:

_____

_____

_____

_____

Listening Time

Listen to an audio book or classical music or ask someone to read a story to you while you color and draw on the next page.

What are you listening to?

_____

Thinking Time!

Can you complete the puzzle?

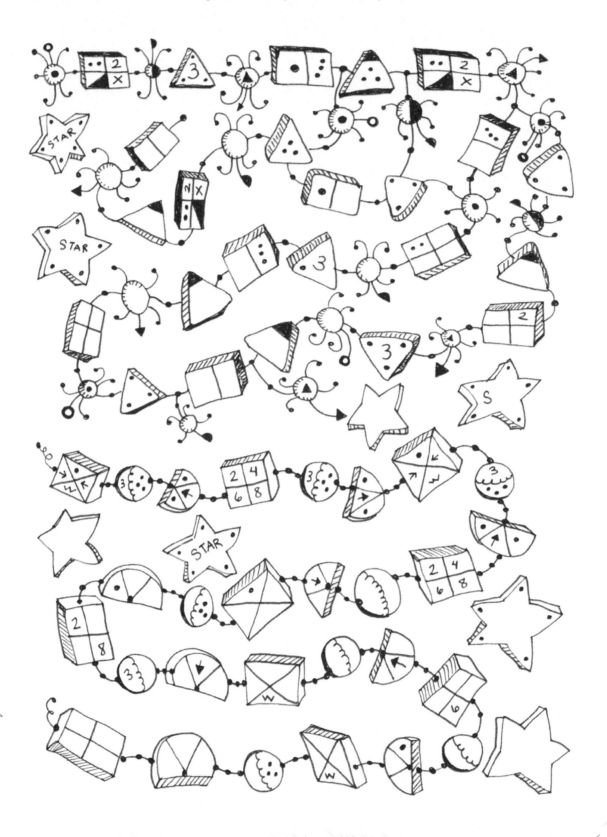

Travel Dreams Geography

Choose any City, any State or any Country:

Where would you like to go?

How far would you travel?

What would you pack?

----

what would you see?

What would you eat?

What is the weather like?

What makes this place unique?

Share an interesting fact:

Draw something you would see in this place:

Priority and Planning

Date:_____

A Quote
_____
_____
_____

To-Do List
_____
_____
_____
_____

My Plans
_____
_____
_____

My Goals
_____
_____
_____

Notes:
_____
_____
_____
_____
_____

Relax and be Creative

Practice working with your colored pencils.

Object Lesson

Look at this picture.

List four things that you understand about the object.

1._____

2._____

3._____

4._____

Just be Creative.

Notes:

_____
_____
_____

Nature Study

Go outside and make a realistic drawing of
something you find in nature.

Reading Time - 1 Hour (Set a timer)

Choose Four Books - Read from each book for 15 minutes.

Copy important words or pictures from each book here:

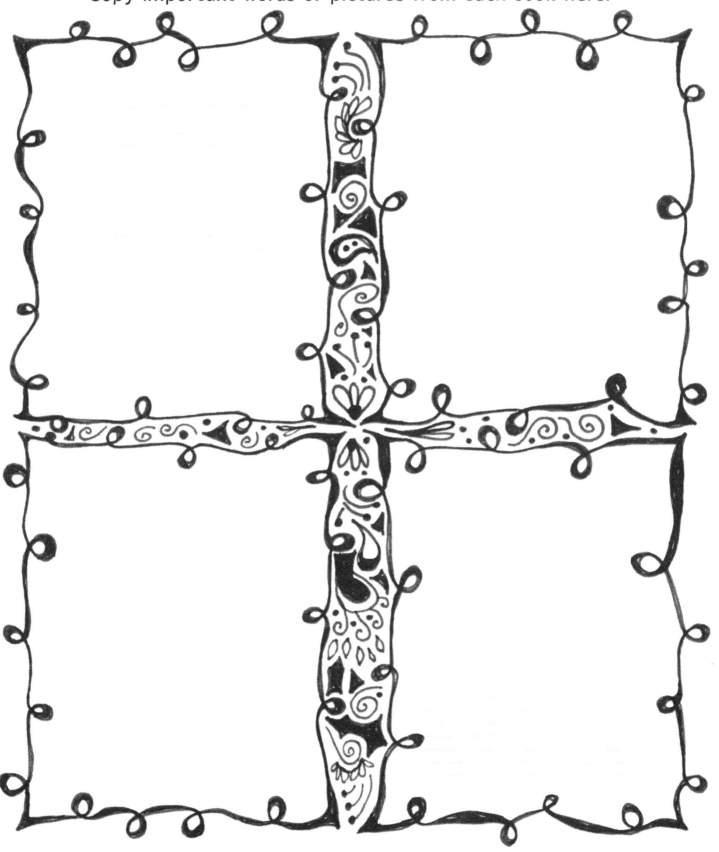

Spelling Time

Find 20 Words with 9 letters each. Look around your house and in your books for words. Write the words here:

_____   _____

_____   _____

_____   _____

_____   _____

_____   _____

_____   _____

_____   _____

_____   _____

_____   _____

Start Time:

Stop Time:

Screen Time!

Watch a Documentary, Educational Program, Movie, or Tutorial.

TITLE: _____

SUBJECT _____

LOCATION: _____

MESSAGE: _____

Rating:

AWFUL

BAD

LAME

YUCKY

OKAY

NICE

GOOD

GREAT

SUPER

Notes:

TITLE:

Draw a Scene from the video:

Use THIS PAGE for Math Practice

Or be creative and design something, like a house! You could make graphs, maps or geometric designs with this graph paper.

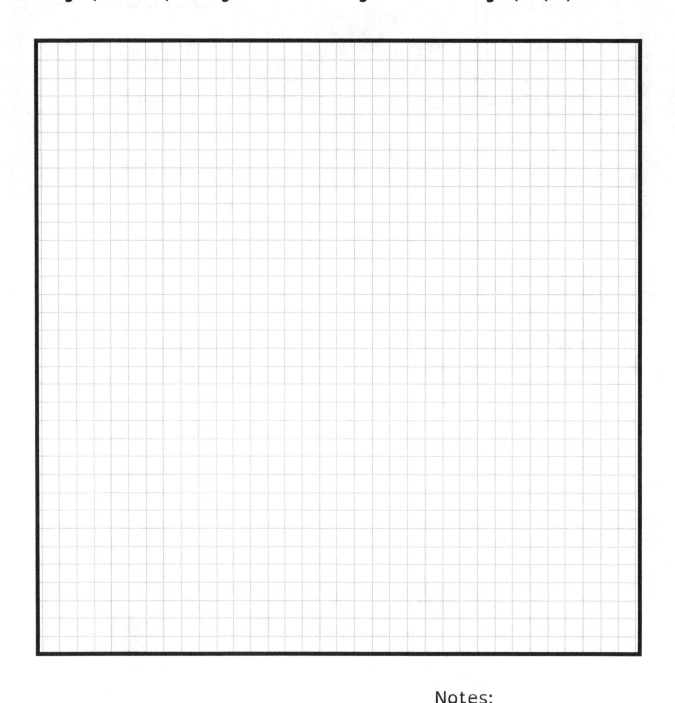

Notes:

_____

_____

_____

_____

World News Today!

Talk to your parents about current events.

Look at a newspaper, news broadcast or website.

Color the countries your learn about.

Tell the news stories with words or pictures.

Book of the Day

Choose a book from your stack that you want to focus on today.

Write and Draw to show what your are learning.

TITLE:_____

Thinking Time!

Can you complete the puzzle?

Travel Dreams Geography

Choose any City, any State or any Country:

Where would you like to go?

How far would you travel?

What would you pack?

----

what would you see?

What would you eat?

What is the weather like?

What makes this place unique?

Share an interesting fact:

Draw something you would see in this place:

Priority and Planning

Date:_____

A Quote
_____
_____
_____

To-Do List
_____
_____
_____
_____

My Plans
_____
_____
_____

My Goals
_____
_____
_____

Notes:
_____
_____
_____
_____

Object Lesson

Look at this picture.

List four things that you understand about the object.

1._____

2._____

3._____

4._____

Just be Creative.

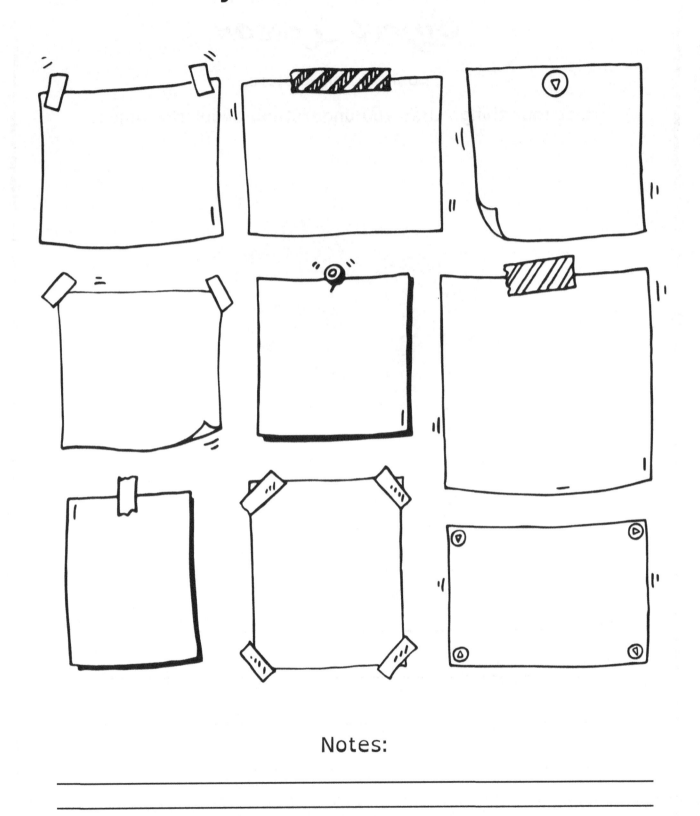

Notes:

_____

_____

_____

Nature Study

Go outside and make a realistic drawing of
something you find in nature.

Reading Time - 1 Hour (Set a timer)

Choose Four Books - Read from each book for 15 minutes.

Copy important words or pictures from each book here:

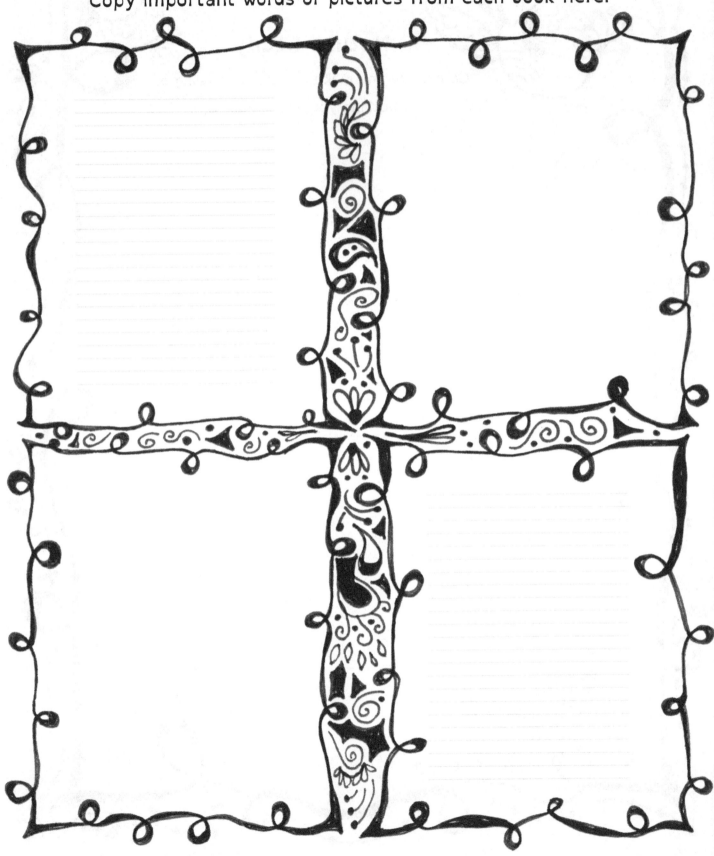

Spelling Time

Find 20 Words with **8** letters each.
Look around your house and in your
books for words. Write the words here:

_____   _____

_____   _____

_____   _____

_____   _____

_____   _____

_____   _____

_____   _____

_____   _____

_____   _____

_____   _____

Start Time:

Stop Time:

Screen Time!

Watch a Documentary, Educational Program, Movie, or Tutorial.

TITLE: _____

SUBJECT _____

LOCATION: _____

MESSAGE: _____

Rating:

AWFUL

BAD

LAME

YUCKY

OKAY

NICE

GOOD

GREAT

SUPER

Notes:

TITLE:

Draw a Scene from the video:

Use THIS PAGE for Math Practice

Or be creative and design something, like a house! You could make graphs, maps or geometric designs with this graph paper.

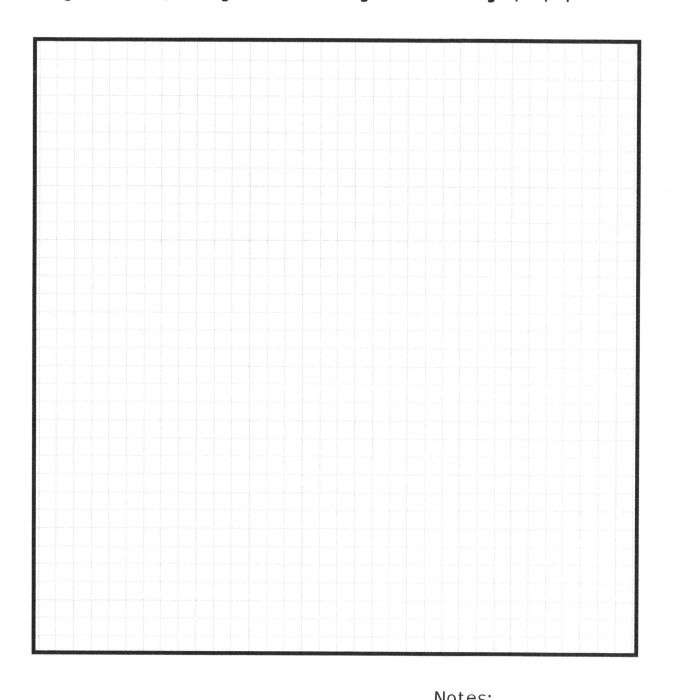

Notes:

_____

_____

_____

_____

Font Writing Practice:

ABCDEFGHIJKLMNOPQRSTUVWXYZ

abcdefghijklmnopqrstuvwxyz

ABCDEFGHIJKLMNOPQRSTUVWXYZ

ABCDEFGHIJKLMNOPQRSTUVWXYZ

Abcdefghijklmnopqrstuvwxyz

Develop Your Own Style

Book of the Day

Choose a book from your stack that you want to focus on today.

Write and Draw to show what your are learning.

TITLE:_____

Thinking Time!

Can you complete the puzzle?

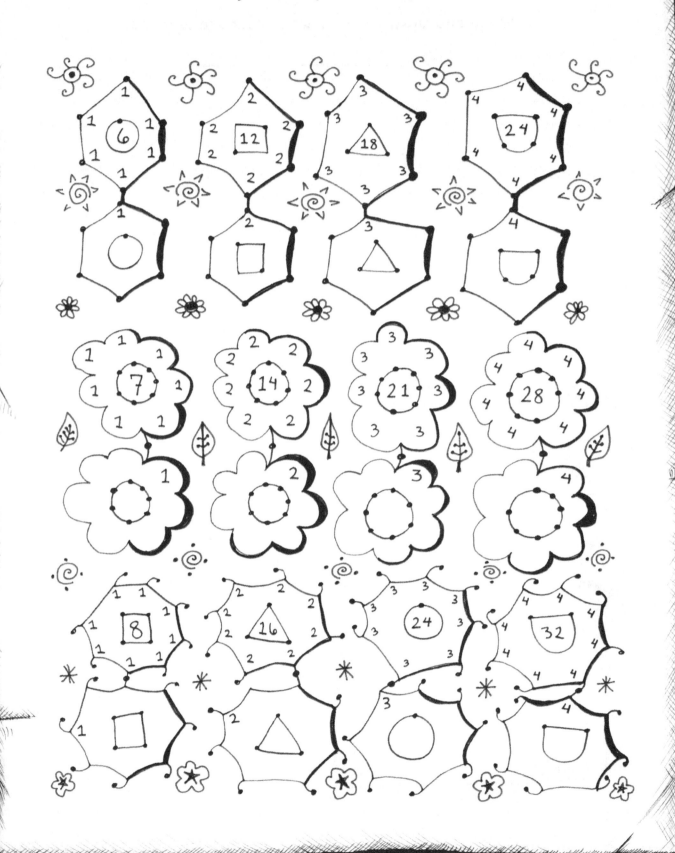

Travel Dreams Geography

Choose any City, any State or any Country:

Where would you like to go?

How far would you travel?

What would you pack?

----

what would you see?

What would you eat?

What is the weather like?

What makes this place unique?

Share an interesting fact:

Draw something you would see in this place:

Priority and Planning

Date:_____

A Quote
_____
_____
_____

To-Do List
_____
_____
_____
_____

My Plans
_____
_____
_____

My Goals
_____
_____
_____

Notes:
_____
_____
_____
_____

Relax and be Creative

Practice working with your colored pencils.

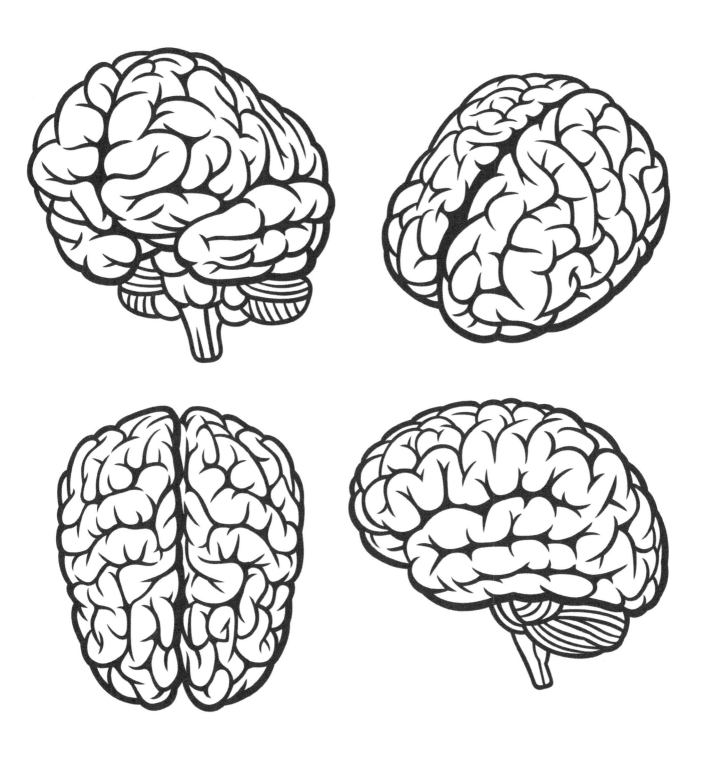

Object Lesson

Look at this picture.

List four things that you understand about the object.

1._____

2._____

3._____

4._____

Just be Creative.

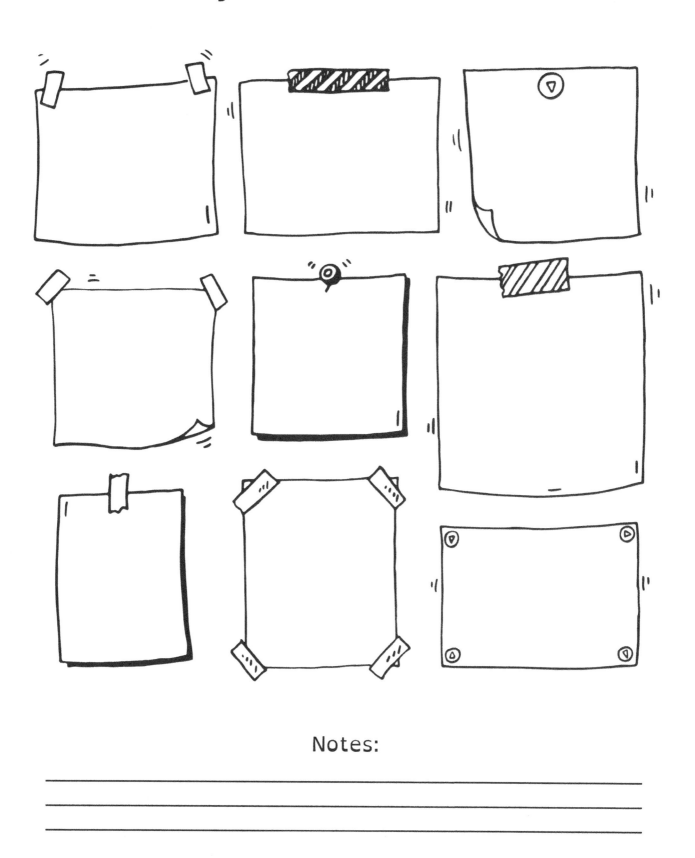

Notes:
_____
_____
_____

Nature Study

Go outside and make a realistic drawing of something you find in nature.

Reading Time - 1 Hour (Set a timer)

Choose Four Books - Read from each book for 15 minutes.

Copy important words or pictures from each book here:

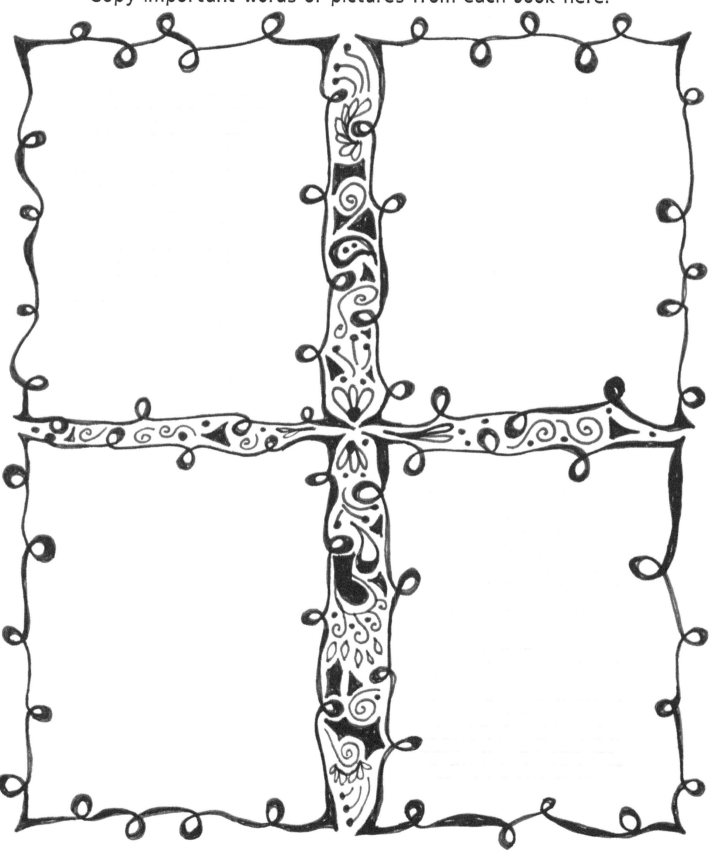

Spelling Time

Find 20 Words with 7 letters each.
Look around your house and in your
books for words. Write the words here:

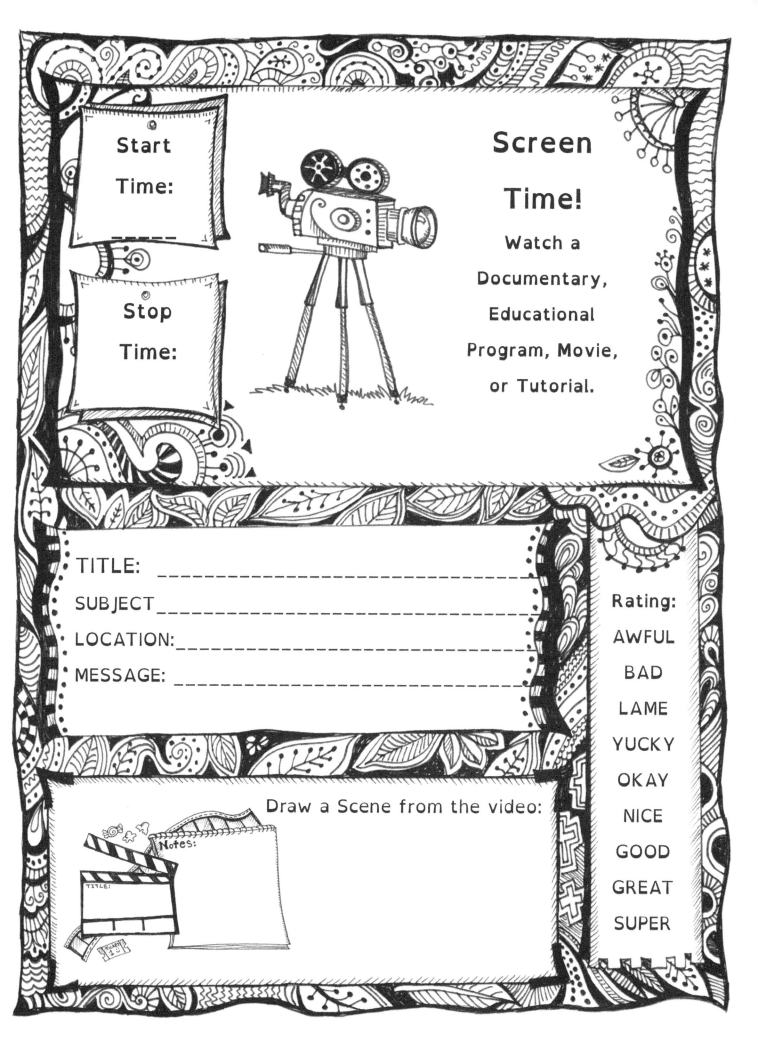

Start Time:

Stop Time:

Screen Time!

Watch a Documentary, Educational Program, Movie, or Tutorial.

TITLE: _____

SUBJECT_____

LOCATION: _____

MESSAGE: _____

Draw a Scene from the video:

Notes:

TITLE:

Rating:

AWFUL

BAD

LAME

YUCKY

OKAY

NICE

GOOD

GREAT

SUPER

Use THIS PAGE for Math Practice

Or be creative and design something, like a house! You could make graphs, maps or geometric designs with this graph paper.

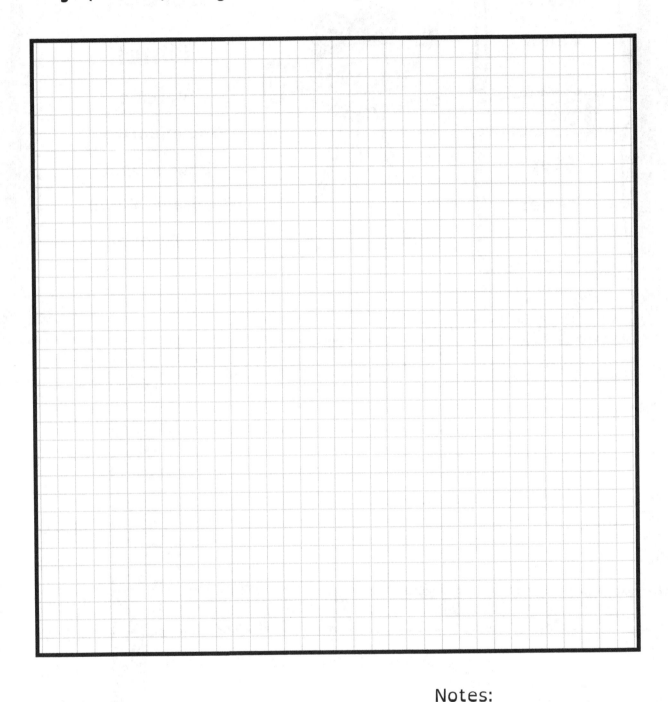

Notes:

_____

_____

_____

_____

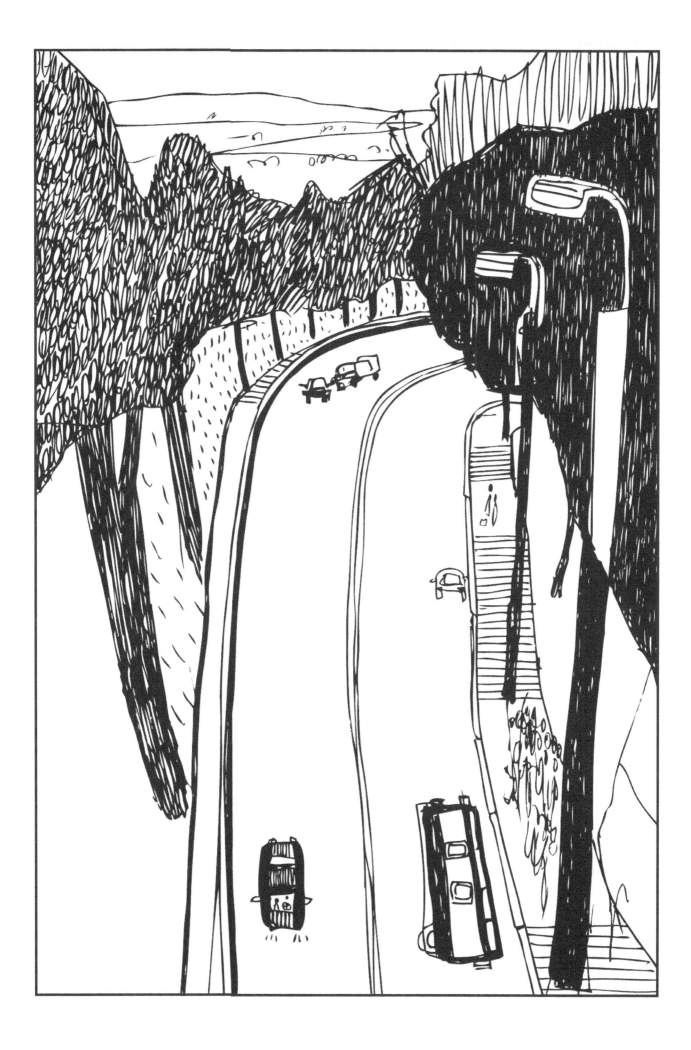

Book of the Day

Choose a book from your stack that you want to focus on today.

Write and Draw to show what your are learning.

TITLE:_____

Thinking Time!

Can you complete the puzzle?

Travel Dreams Geography

Choose any City, any State or any Country:

Where would you like to go?

How far would you travel?

What would you pack?

----

what would you see?

What would you eat?

What is the weather like?

What makes this place unique?

Share an interesting fact:

Draw something you would see in this place:

Priority and Planning

Date:_____

A Quote

_____
_____
_____

To-Do List

_____
_____
_____
_____

My Plans

_____
_____
_____

My Goals

_____
_____
_____

Notes:

_____
_____
_____
_____
_____

Object Lesson

Look at this picture.

List four things that you understand about the object.

1._____

2._____

3._____

4._____

Just be Creative.

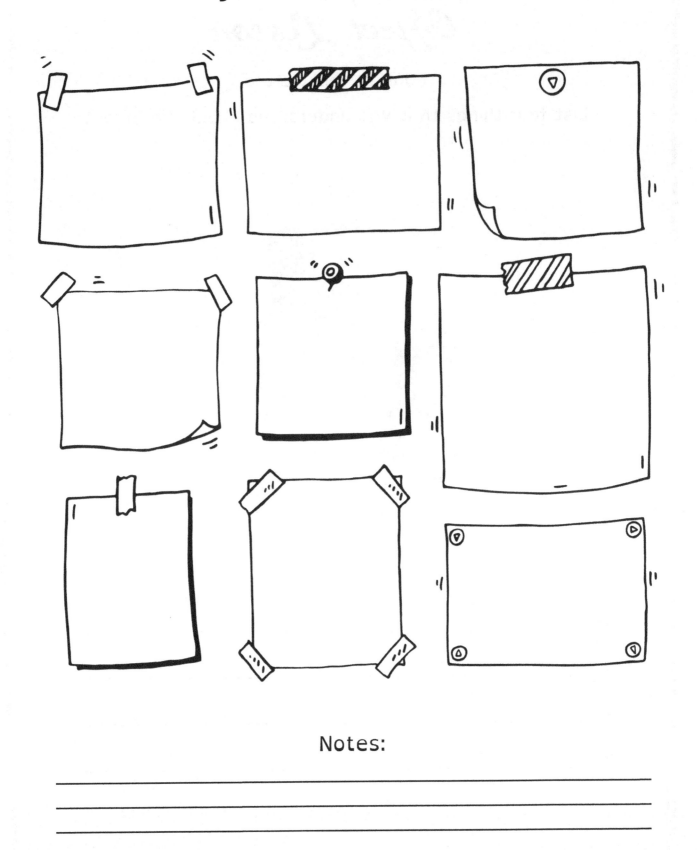

Notes:

Nature Study

Go outside and make a realistic drawing of something you find in nature.

Reading Time - 1 Hour (Set a timer)

Choose Four Books - Read from each book for 15 minutes.

Copy important words or pictures from each book here:

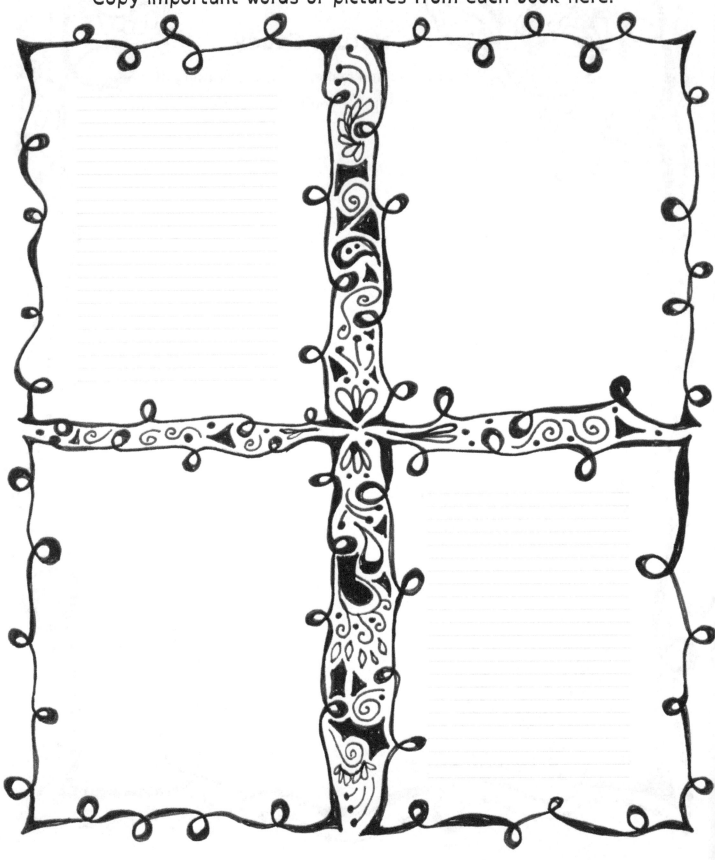

Spelling Time

Find 20 Words with 6 letters each.
Look around your house and in your
books for words. Write the words here:

Start Time:

_ _ _ _ _

Stop Time:

Screen Time!

Watch a Documentary, Educational Program, Movie, or Tutorial.

TITLE: _____

SUBJECT _____

LOCATION: _____

MESSAGE: _____

Rating:

AWFUL

BAD

LAME

YUCKY

OKAY

NICE

GOOD

GREAT

SUPER

Notes:

TITLE:

Draw a Scene from the video:

Use THIS PAGE for Math Practice

Or be creative and design something, like a house! You could make graphs, maps or geometric designs with this graph paper.

Notes:

_____

_____

_____

_____

Book of the Day

Choose a book from your stack that you want to focus on today.

Write and Draw to show what your are learning.

TITLE:_____

Thinking Time!

Can you complete the puzzle?

Travel Dreams Geography

Choose any City, any State or any Country:

Where would you like to go?

_____

How far would you travel?

_____

What would you pack?

_____

what would you see?

_____

What would you eat?

_____

What is the weather like?

_____

What makes this place unique?

_____

Share an interesting fact:

_____

Draw something you would see in this place:

Priority and Planning

Date:_____

A Quote

_____
_____
_____

To-Do List

_____
_____
_____
_____

My Plans

_____
_____
_____

My Goals

_____
_____
_____

Notes:

_____
_____
_____
_____
_____

Relax and be Creative

Practice working with your colored pencils.

Object Lesson

Look at this picture.

List four things that you understand about the object.

1._____

2._____

3._____

4._____

Journal

A Day in My Life

Nature Study

Go outside and make a realistic drawing of
something you find in nature.

Reading Time - 1 Hour (Set a timer)

Choose Four Books - Read from each book for 15 minutes.

Copy important words or pictures from each book here:

Spelling Time

5

Find 20 Words with _____ letters each.

Look around your house and in your

books for words. Write the words here:

Start Time: _____

Stop Time:

Screen Time!

Watch a Documentary, Educational Program, Movie, or Tutorial.

TITLE: _____

SUBJECT _____

LOCATION: _____

MESSAGE: _____

Rating:

AWFUL

BAD

LAME

YUCKY

OKAY

NICE

GOOD

GREAT

SUPER

Draw a Scene from the video:

Notes:

TITLE:

Use THIS PAGE for Math Practice

Or be creative and design something, like a house! You could make graphs, maps or geometric designs with this graph paper.

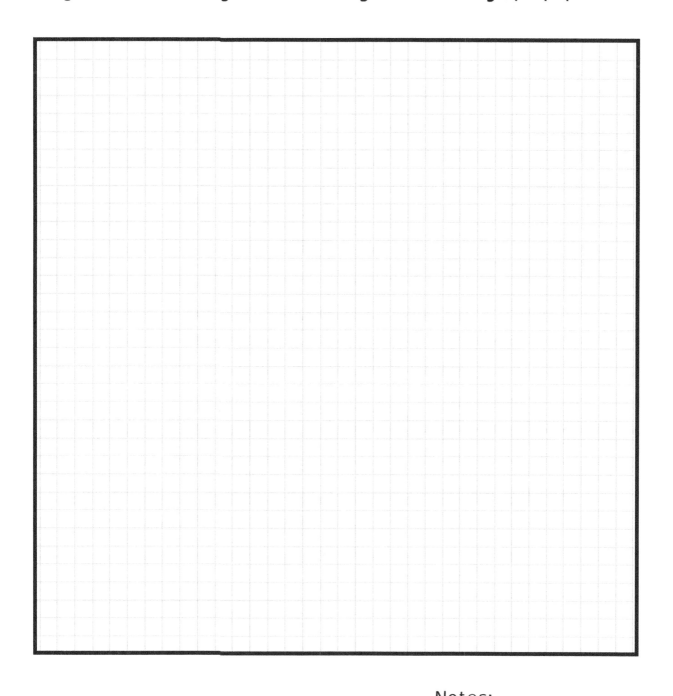

Notes:

_____

_____

_____

_____

World News Today!

Talk to your parents about current events.

Look at a newspaper, news broadcast or website.

Color the countries your learn about.

Tell the news stories with words or pictures.

Book of the Day

Choose a book from your stack that you want to focus on today.

Write and Draw to show what your are learning.

TITLE:_____

Thinking Time!

Can you complete the puzzle?

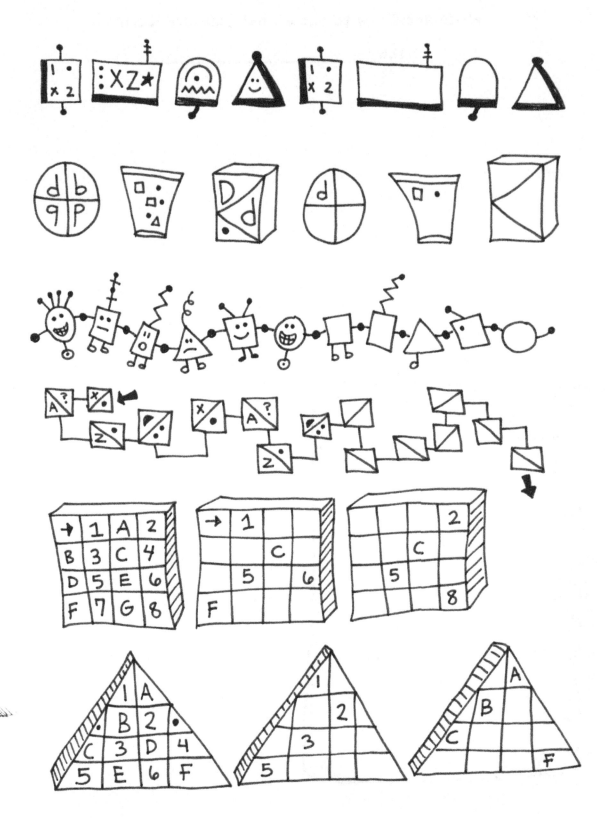

Travel Dreams Geography

Choose any City, any State or any Country:

Where would you like to go?

How far would you travel?

What would you pack?

----

what would you see?

What would you eat?

What is the weather like?

What makes this place unique?

Share an interesting fact:

Draw something you would see in this place:

Priority and Planning

Date:_____

A Quote
_____
_____
_____

To-Do List
_____
_____
_____

My Plans
_____
_____
_____

My Goals
_____
_____
_____

Notes:
_____
_____
_____
_____
_____

Relax and be Creative

Practice working with your colored pencils.

Object Lesson

Look at this picture.

List four things that you understand about the object.

1. _____

2. _____

3. _____

4. _____

Just be Creative.

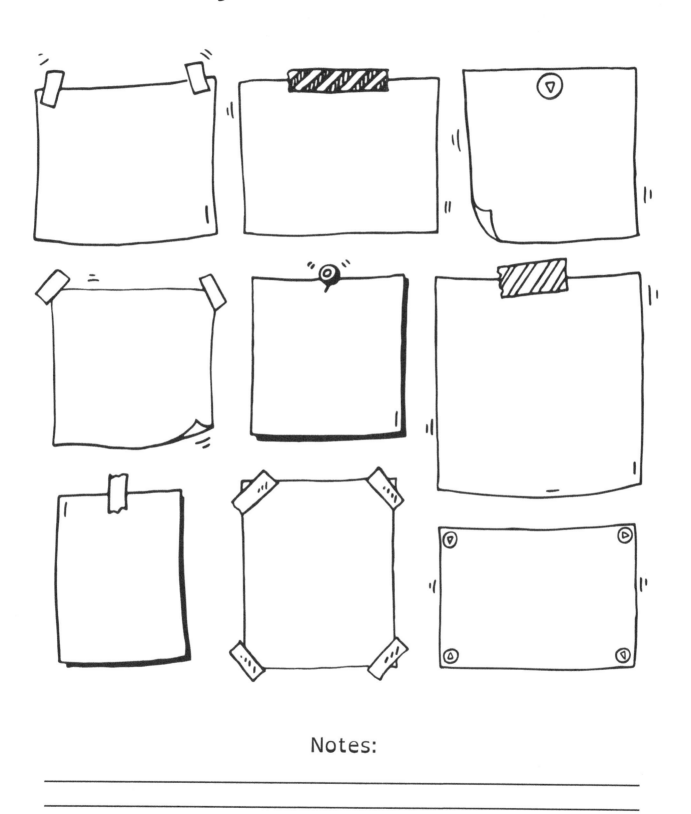

Notes:

_____

_____

_____

Nature Study

Go outside and make a realistic drawing of something you find in nature.

Reading Time - 1 Hour (Set a timer)

Choose Four Books - Read from each book for 15 minutes.

Copy important words or pictures from each book here:

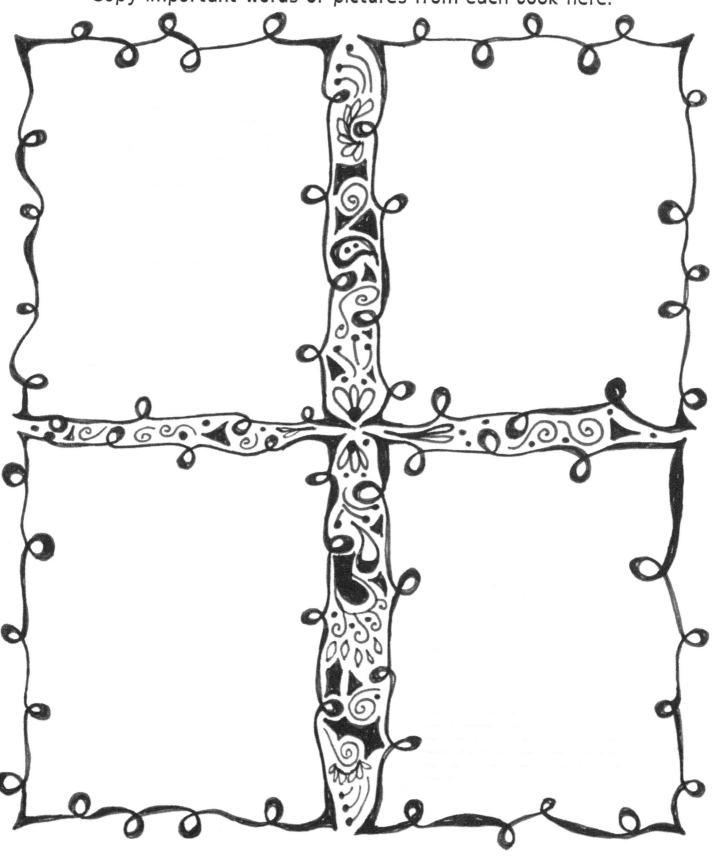

Spelling Time

Find 20 Words with 9 letters each.
Look around your house and in your
books for words. Write the words here:

Start Time: _____

Stop Time: _____

Screen Time!

Watch a Documentary, Educational Program, Movie, or Tutorial.

TITLE: _____

SUBJECT _____

LOCATION: _____

MESSAGE: _____

Rating:

AWFUL

BAD

LAME

YUCKY

OKAY

NICE

GOOD

GREAT

SUPER

Notes:

TITLE:

Draw a Scene from the video:

Use THIS PAGE for Math Practice

Or be creative and design something, like a house! You could make graphs, maps or geometric designs with this graph paper.

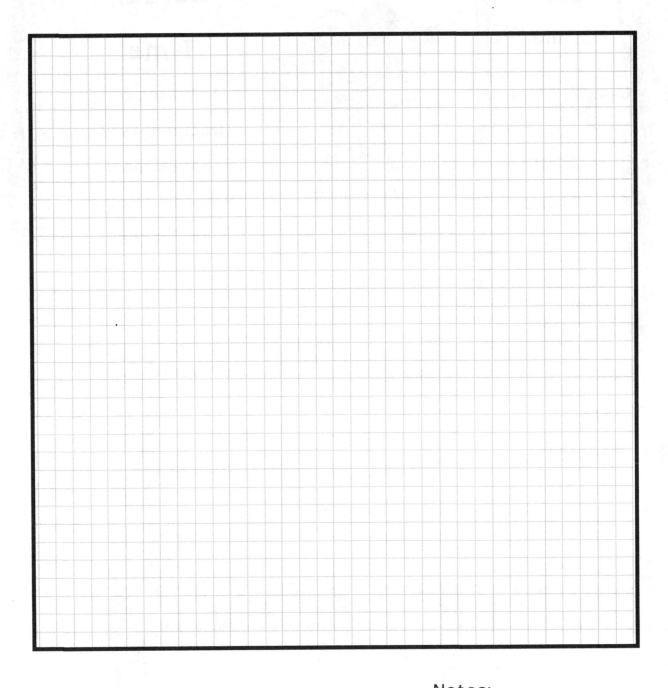

Notes:

_____

_____

_____

_____

Font Writing Practice:

ABCDEFGHIJKLMNOPQRSTUVWXYZ

abcdefghijklmnopqrstuvwxyz

ABCDEFGHIJKLMNOPQRSTUVWXYZ

ABCDEFGHIJKLMNOPQRSTUVWXYZ

Abcdefghijklmnopqrstuvwxyz

Develop Your Own Style

Book of the Day

Choose a book from your stack that you want to focus on today.

Write and Draw to show what your are learning.

TITLE:_____

Thinking Time!

Can you complete the puzzle?

Key:
- ☺ = ○
- 🧍 = 1
- 🌻 = 2
- 🌙 = 3
- ⭐ = 4
- ☀ = 5
- 🌳 = 6
- ☕ = 7
- 🧁 = 8
- 🎲 = 9

12   15   18   24   21

16   24   32   28   36

25   30   45   35   40

36   42   54   48   24

Travel Dreams Geography

Choose any City, any State or any Country:

Where would you like to go?

How far would you travel?

What would you pack?

----

what would you see?

What would you eat?

What is the weather like?

What makes this place unique?

Share an interesting fact:

Draw something you would see in this place:

Priority and Planning

Date:_____

A Quote

_____
_____
_____

To-Do List

_____
_____
_____
_____

My Plans

_____
_____
_____

My Goals

_____
_____
_____

Notes:

_____
_____
_____
_____
_____

Relax and be Creative

Practice working with your colored pencils.

Object Lesson

Look at this picture.

List four things that you understand about the object.

1._____

2._____

3._____

4._____

Nature Study

Go outside and make a realistic drawing of
something you find in nature.

Reading Time - 1 Hour (Set a timer)

Choose Four Books - Read from each book for 15 minutes.

Copy important words or pictures from each book here:

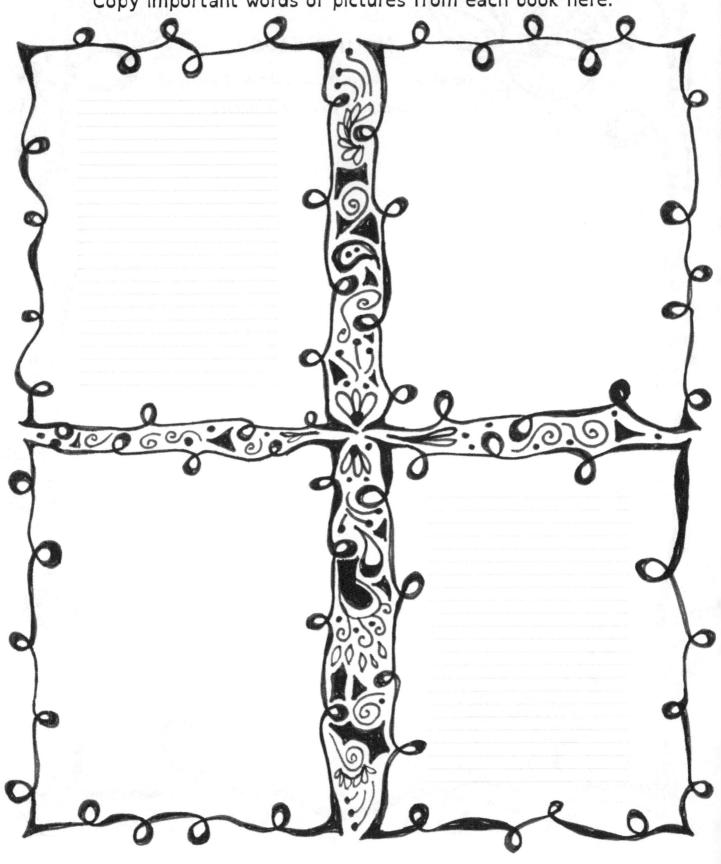

Spelling Time

Find 20 Words with **8** letters each.
Look around your house and in your
books for words. Write the words here:

Start Time:

Stop Time:

Screen Time!

Watch a Documentary, Educational Program, Movie, or Tutorial.

TITLE: _____

SUBJECT _____

LOCATION: _____

MESSAGE: _____

Rating:

AWFUL

BAD

LAME

YUCKY

OKAY

NICE

GOOD

GREAT

SUPER

Draw a Scene from the video:

Notes:

TITLE:

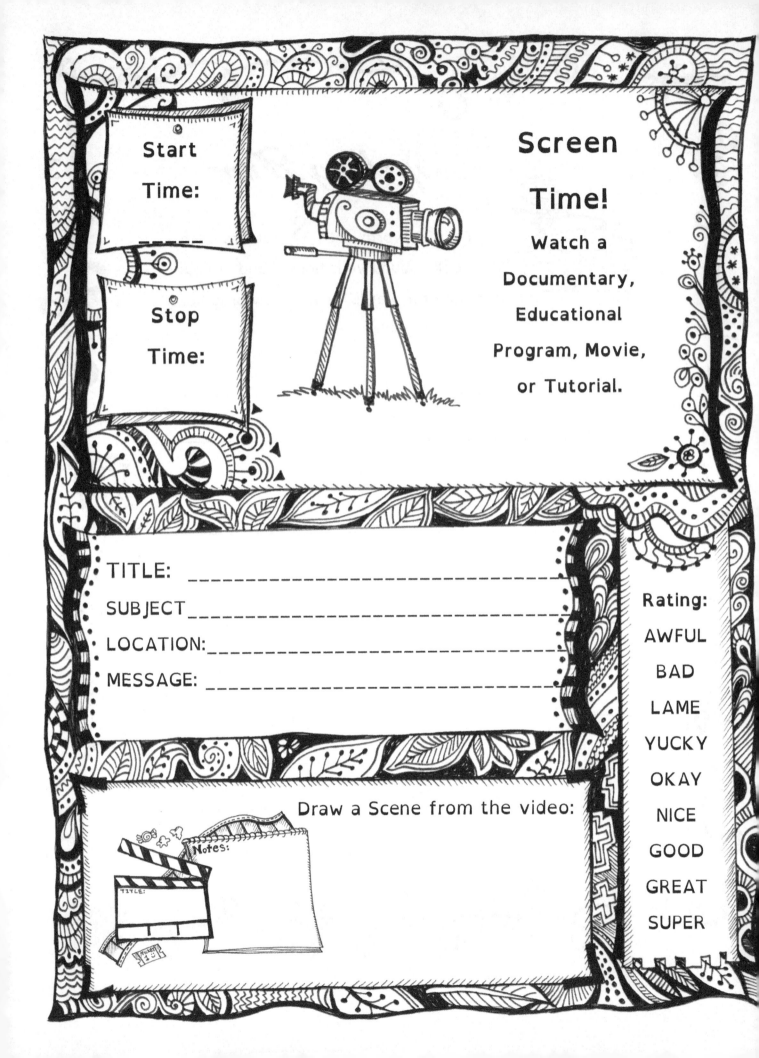

Use THIS PAGE for Math Practice

Or be creative and design something, like a house! You could make graphs, maps or geometric designs with this graph paper.

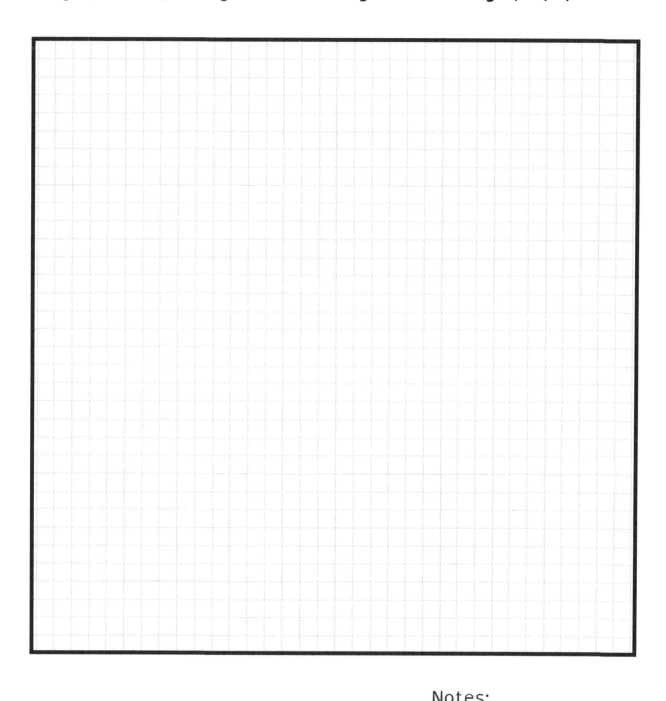

Notes:

_____

_____

_____

_____

Listening Time

Listen to an audio book or classical music or
ask someone to read a story to you while
you color and draw on the next page.

What are you listening to?

_____

Thinking Time!

Can you complete the puzzle?

Travel Dreams Geography

Choose any City, any State or any Country:

Where would you like to go?

How far would you travel?

What would you pack?

----

what would you see?

What would you eat?

What is the weather like?

What makes this place unique?

Share an interesting fact:

Draw something you would see in this place:

Priority and Planning

Date:_____

A Quote

_____
_____
_____
_____

To-Do List

_____
_____
_____
_____

My Plans

_____
_____
_____

My Goals

_____
_____
_____

Notes:

_____
_____
_____
_____
_____

Relax and be Creative

Practice working with your colored pencils.

Object Lesson

Look at this picture.

List four things that you understand about the object.

1. _____

2. _____

3. _____

4. _____

Just be Creative.

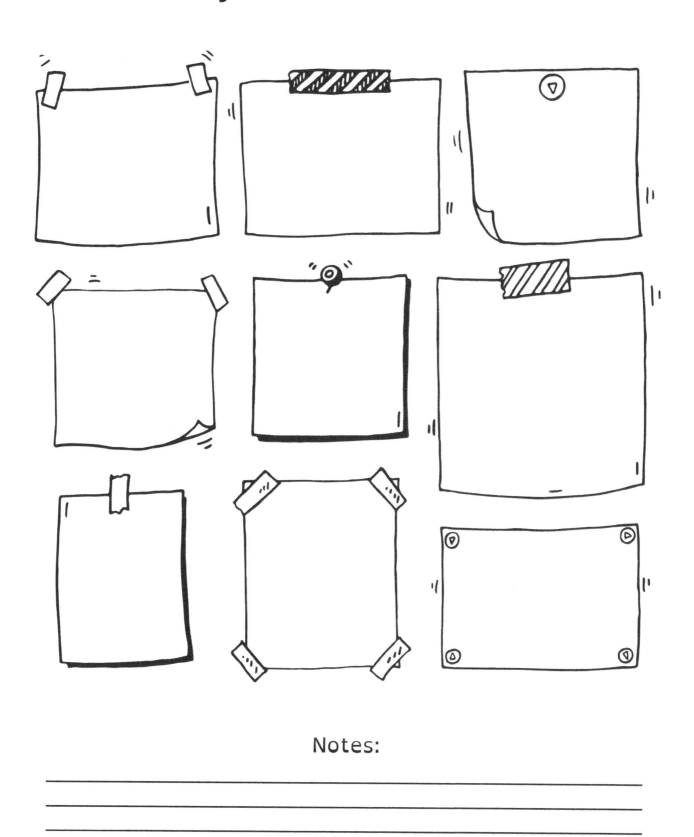

Notes:

Nature Study

Go outside and make a realistic drawing of something you find in nature.

Reading Time - 1 Hour (Set a timer)

Choose Four Books - Read from each book for 15 minutes.

Copy important words or pictures from each book here:

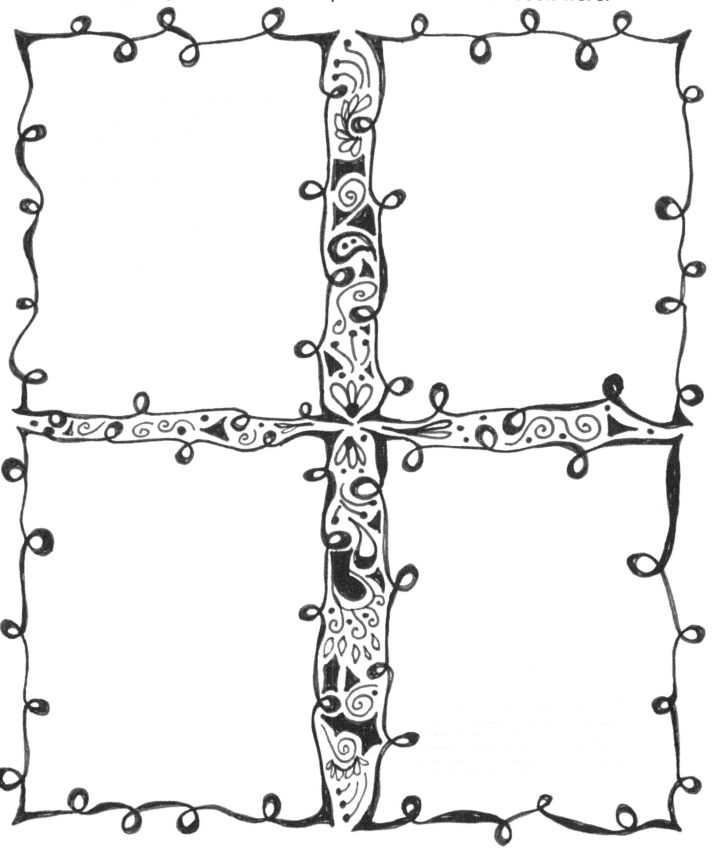

Spelling Time

Find 20 Words with **7** letters each.
Look around your house and in your
books for words. Write the words here:

Start Time:

Stop Time:

Screen Time!

Watch a Documentary, Educational Program, Movie, or Tutorial.

TITLE: _____

SUBJECT _____

LOCATION: _____

MESSAGE: _____

Rating:

AWFUL

BAD

LAME

YUCKY

OKAY

NICE

GOOD

GREAT

SUPER

Notes:

TITLE:

Draw a Scene from the video:

Use THIS PAGE for Math Practice

Or be creative and design something, like a house! You could make graphs, maps or geometric designs with this graph paper.

Notes:

_____

_____

_____

_____

Book of the Day

Choose a book from your stack that you want to focus on today.

Write and Draw to show what your are learning.

TITLE:_____

Thinking Time!

Can you complete the puzzle?

Travel Dreams Geography

Choose any City, any State or any Country:

Where would you like to go?

How far would you travel?

What would you pack?

----

what would you see?

What would you eat?

What is the weather like?

What makes this place unique?

Share an interesting fact:

Draw something you would see in this place:

Priority and Planning

Date:_____

A Quote

_____
_____
_____
_____

To-Do List

_____
_____
_____
_____

My Plans

_____
_____
_____

My Goals

_____
_____
_____

Notes:

_____
_____
_____
_____

Relax and be Creative

Practice working with your colored pencils.

Object Lesson

Look at this picture.

List four things that you understand about the object.

1._____

2._____

3._____

4._____

Journal

A Day in My Life

Nature Study

Go outside and make a realistic drawing of
something you find in nature.

Reading Time - 1 Hour (Set a timer)

Choose Four Books - Read from each book for 15 minutes.

Copy important words or pictures from each book here:

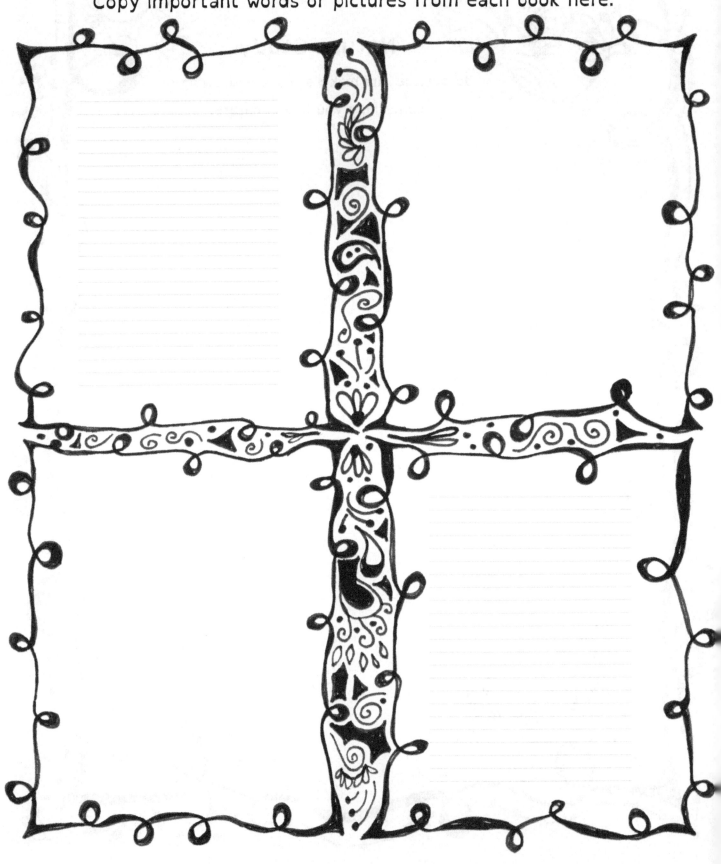

Spelling Time

Find 20 Words with **4** letters each.
Look around your house and in your
books for words. Write the words here:

Start Time:

Stop Time:

Screen Time!

Watch a Documentary, Educational Program, Movie, or Tutorial.

TITLE: _____

SUBJECT_____

LOCATION: _____

MESSAGE: _____

Rating:

AWFUL

BAD

LAME

YUCKY

OKAY

NICE

GOOD

GREAT

SUPER

Draw a Scene from the video:

Notes:

TITLE:

Use THIS PAGE for Math Practice

Or be creative and design something, like a house! You could make graphs, maps or geometric designs with this graph paper.

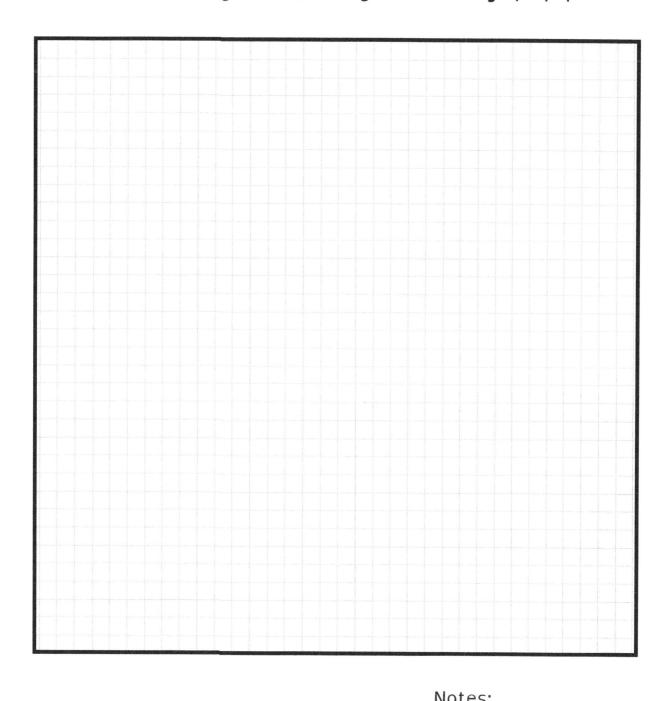

Notes:

_____

_____

_____

_____

Book of the Day

Choose a book from your stack that you want to focus on today.

Write and Draw to show what your are learning.

TITLE:_____

Thinking Time!

Can you complete the puzzle?

Travel Dreams Geography

Choose any City, any State or any Country:

Where would you like to go?

How far would you travel?

What would you pack?

----

what would you see?

What would you eat?

What is the weather like?

What makes this place unique?

Share an interesting fact:

Draw something you would see in this place:

Priority and Planning

Date:_____

A Quote

_____
_____
_____

To-Do List

_____
_____
_____

My Plans

_____
_____
_____

My Goals

_____
_____

Notes:

_____
_____
_____
_____
_____

Relax and be Creative

Practice working with your colored pencils.

Object Lesson

Look at this picture.

List four things that you understand about the object.

1._____

2._____

3._____

4._____

Just be Creative.

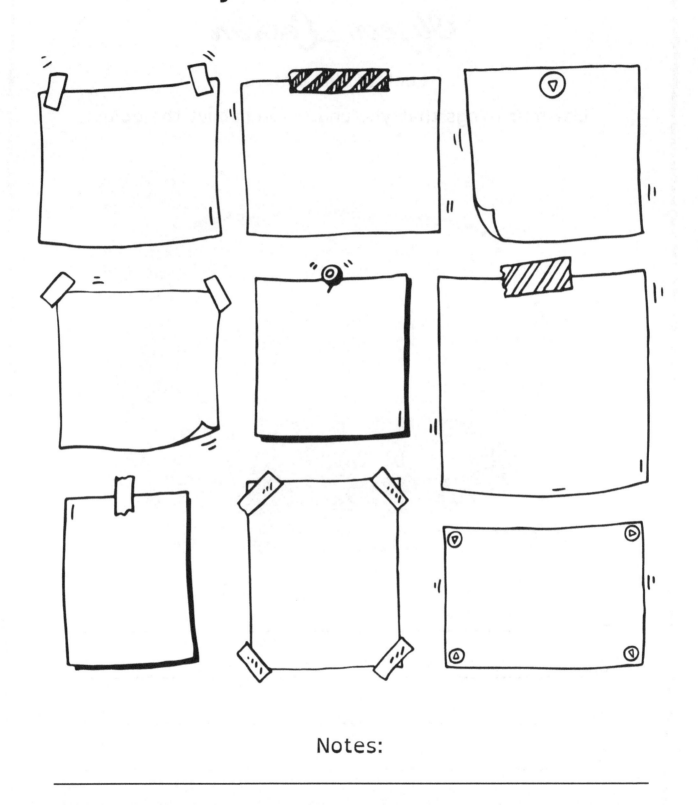

Notes:

_____

_____

_____

Nature Study

Go outside and make a realistic drawing of
something you find in nature.

Reading Time - 1 Hour (Set a timer)

Choose Four Books - Read from each book for 15 minutes.

Copy important words or pictures from each book here:

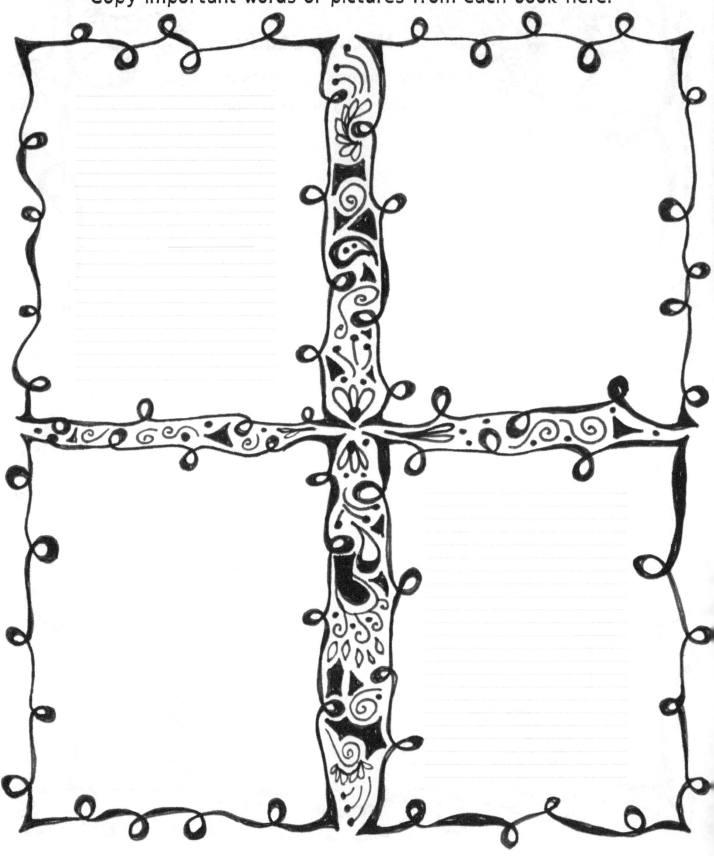

Spelling Time

Find 20 Words with 9 letters each.
Look around your house and in your
books for words. Write the words here:

Start Time:

Stop Time:

Screen Time!

Watch a Documentary, Educational Program, Movie, or Tutorial.

TITLE: _____

SUBJECT _____

LOCATION: _____

MESSAGE: _____

Rating:

AWFUL

BAD

LAME

YUCKY

OKAY

NICE

GOOD

GREAT

SUPER

Draw a Scene from the video:

Notes:

TITLE:

Use THIS PAGE for Math Practice

Or be creative and design something, like a house! You could make graphs, maps or geometric designs with this graph paper.

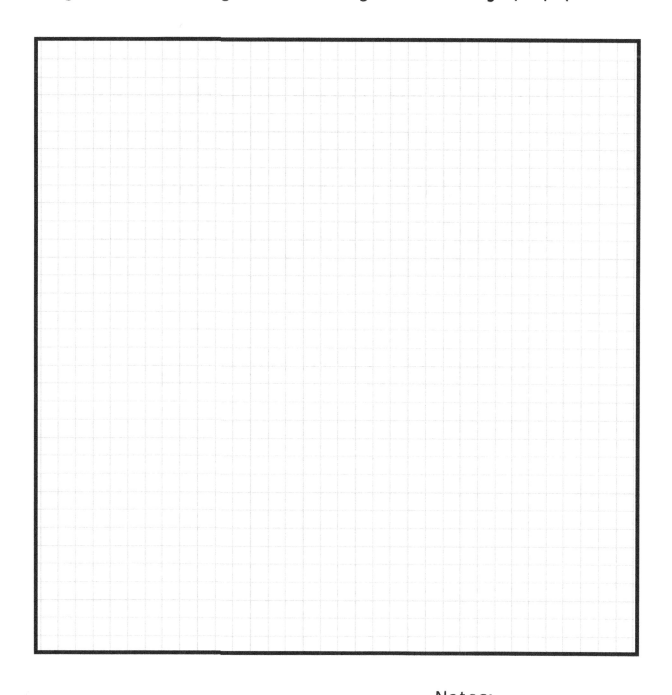

Notes:

_____

_____

_____

_____

Font Writing Practice:

ABCDEFGHIJKLMNOPQRSTUVWXYZ

abcdefghijklmnopqrstuvwxyz

ABCDEFGHIJKLMNOPQRSTUVWXYZ

ABCDEFGHIJKLMNOPQRSTUVWXYZ

Abcdefghijklmnopqrstuvwxyz

Develop Your Own Style

Book of the Day

Choose a book from your stack that you want to focus on today.

Write and Draw to show what your are learning.

TITLE:_____

Travel Dreams Geography

Choose any City, any State or any Country:

Where would you like to go?

How far would you travel?

What would you pack?

----

what would you see?

What would you eat?

What is the weather like?

What makes this place unique?

Share an interesting fact:

Draw something you would see in this place:

Priority and Planning

Date:_____

A Quote

_____

_____

_____

_____

To-Do List

_____

_____

_____

_____

My Plans

_____

_____

_____

_____

My Goals

_____

_____

_____

_____

Notes:

_____

_____

_____

_____

_____

Relax and be Creative

Practice working with your colored pencils.

Object Lesson

Look at this picture.

List four things that you understand about the object.

1._____

2._____

3._____

4._____

Just be Creative.

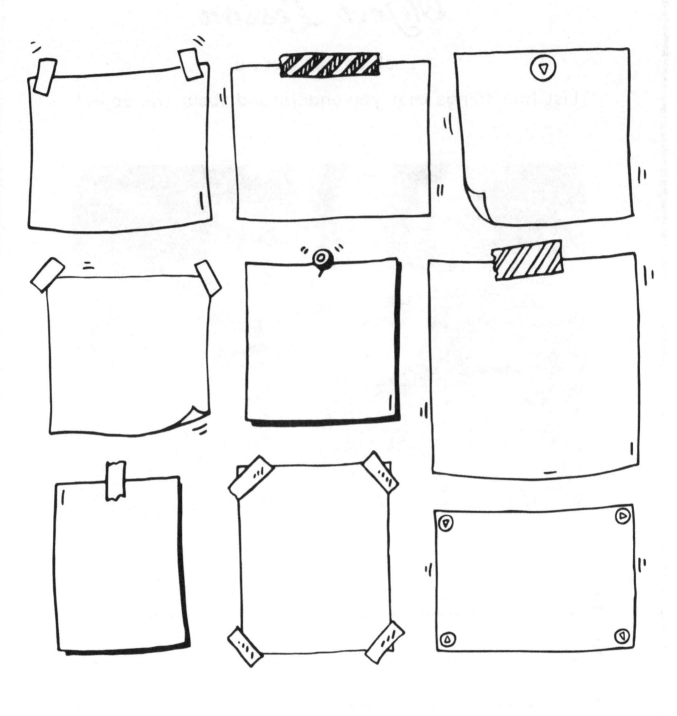

Notes:

_____

_____

_____

Nature Study

Go outside and make a realistic drawing of
something you find in nature.

Reading Time - 1 Hour (Set a timer)

Choose Four Books - Read from each book for 15 minutes.

Copy important words or pictures from each book here:

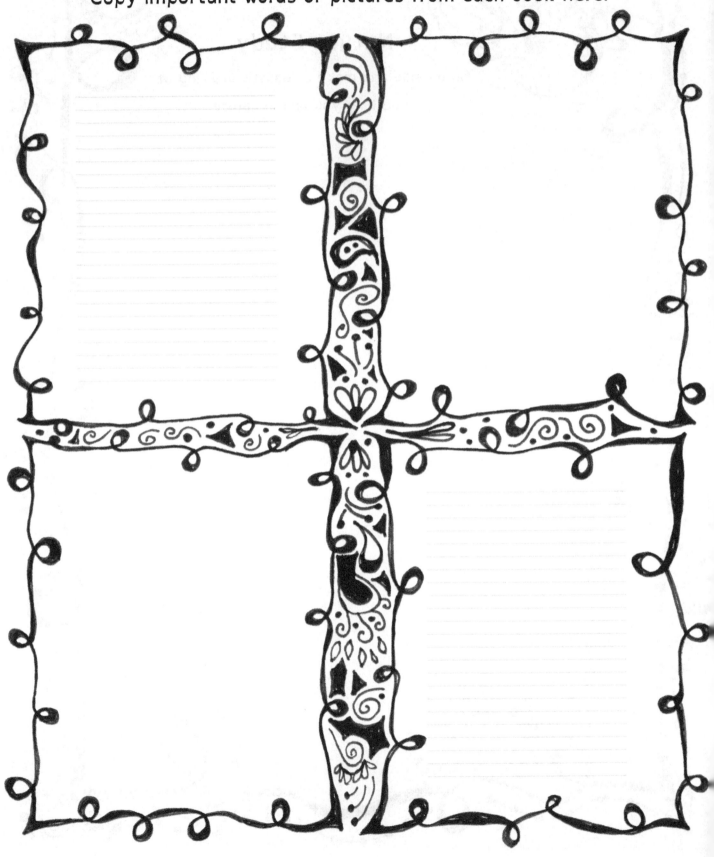

Spelling Time

6

Find 20 Words with   letters each.
Look around your house and in your
books for words. Write the words here:

_____   _____

_____   _____

_____   _____

_____   _____

_____   _____

_____   _____

_____   _____

_____   _____

_____   _____

_____   _____

Start Time:

Stop Time:

Screen Time!

Watch a Documentary, Educational Program, Movie, or Tutorial.

TITLE: _____

SUBJECT _____

LOCATION: _____

MESSAGE: _____

Rating:

AWFUL

BAD

LAME

YUCKY

OKAY

NICE

GOOD

GREAT

SUPER

Draw a Scene from the video:

Notes:

TITLE:

Use THIS PAGE for Math Practice

Or be creative and design something, like a house! You could make graphs, maps or geometric designs with this graph paper.

Notes:

_____

_____

_____

_____

World News Today!

Talk to your parents about current events.

Look at a newspaper, news broadcast or website.

Color the countries your learn about.

Tell the news stories with words or pictures.

Book of the Day

Choose a book from your stack that you want to focus on today.

Write and Draw to show what your are learning.

TITLE:_____

Thinking Time!

Can you complete the puzzle?

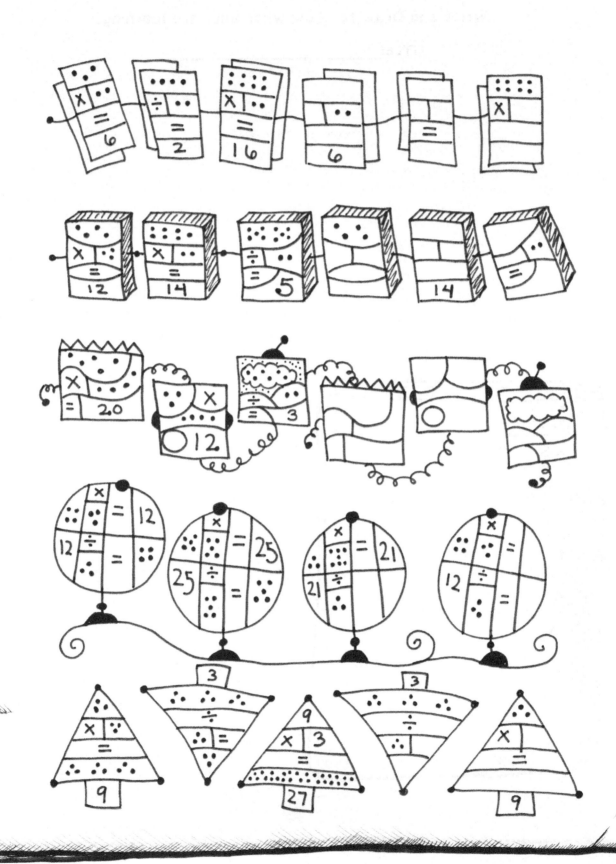

Travel Dreams Geography

Choose any City, any State or any Country:

Where would you like to go?

How far would you travel?

What would you pack?

----

what would you see?

What would you eat?

What is the weather like?

What makes this place unique?

Share an interesting fact:

Draw something you would see in this place:

Priority and Planning

Date:_____

A Quote

_____
_____
_____
_____

To-Do List

_____
_____
_____
_____

My Plans

_____
_____
_____

My Goals

_____
_____
_____

Notes:

_____
_____
_____
_____

Relax and be Creative

Practice working with your colored pencils.

Object Lesson

Look at this picture.

List four things that you understand about the object.

1. _____

2. _____

3. _____

4. _____

Painting by George Dunlop Leslie

Just be Creative.

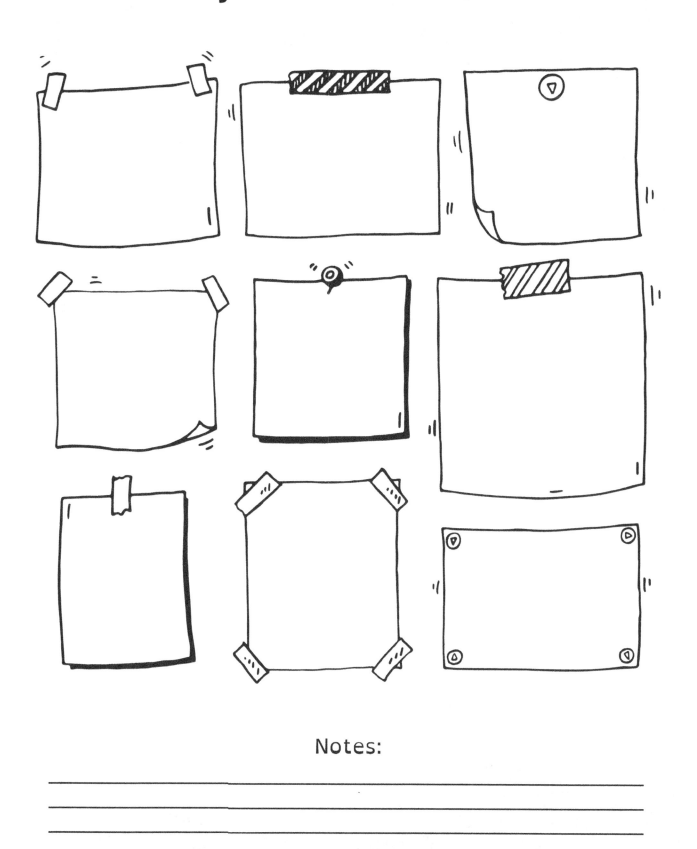

Notes:
_____
_____
_____

Nature Study

Go outside and make a realistic drawing of
something you find in nature.

Reading Time - 1 Hour (Set a timer)

Choose Four Books - Read from each book for 15 minutes.

Copy important words or pictures from each book here:

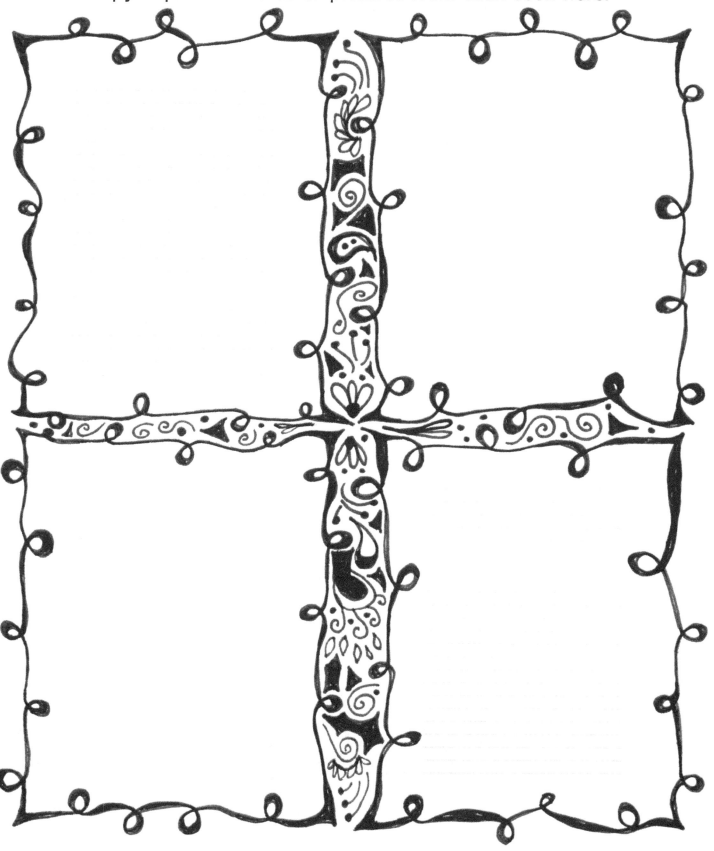

Spelling Time

Find 20 Words with 7 letters each.
Look around your house and in your
books for words. Write the words here:

Start Time: _____

Stop Time:

Screen Time!

Watch a Documentary, Educational Program, Movie, or Tutorial.

TITLE: _____

SUBJECT_____

LOCATION:_____

MESSAGE: _____

Rating:

AWFUL

BAD

LAME

YUCKY

OKAY

NICE

GOOD

GREAT

SUPER

Notes:

TITLE:

Draw a Scene from the video:

Use THIS PAGE for Math Practice

Or be creative and design something, like a house! You could make graphs, maps or geometric designs with this graph paper.

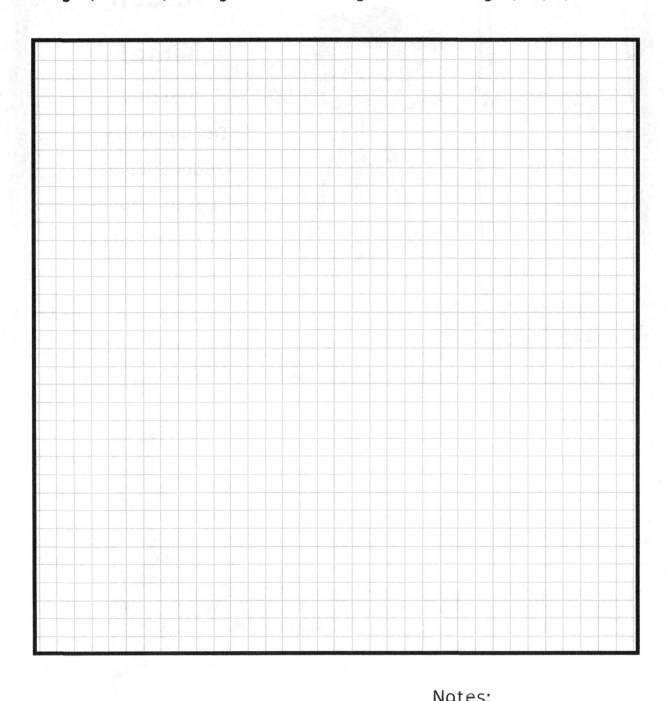

Notes:

_____

_____

_____

_____

Book of the Day

Choose a book from your stack that you want to focus on today.

Write and Draw to show what your are learning.

TITLE:_____

Thinking Time!

Can you complete the puzzle?

Travel Dreams Geography

Choose any City, any State or any Country:

Where would you like to go?

How far would you travel?

What would you pack?

----

what would you see?

What would you eat?

What is the weather like?

What makes this place unique?

Share an interesting fact:

Draw something you would see in this place:

Priority and Planning

Date:_____

A Quote

_____
_____
_____

To-Do List

_____
_____
_____
_____

My Plans

_____
_____
_____

My Goals

_____
_____
_____

Notes:

_____
_____
_____
_____
_____

Relax and be Creative

Practice working with your colored pencils.

Object Lesson

Look at this picture.

List four things that you understand about the object.

1. _____

2. _____

3. _____

4. _____

Just be Creative.

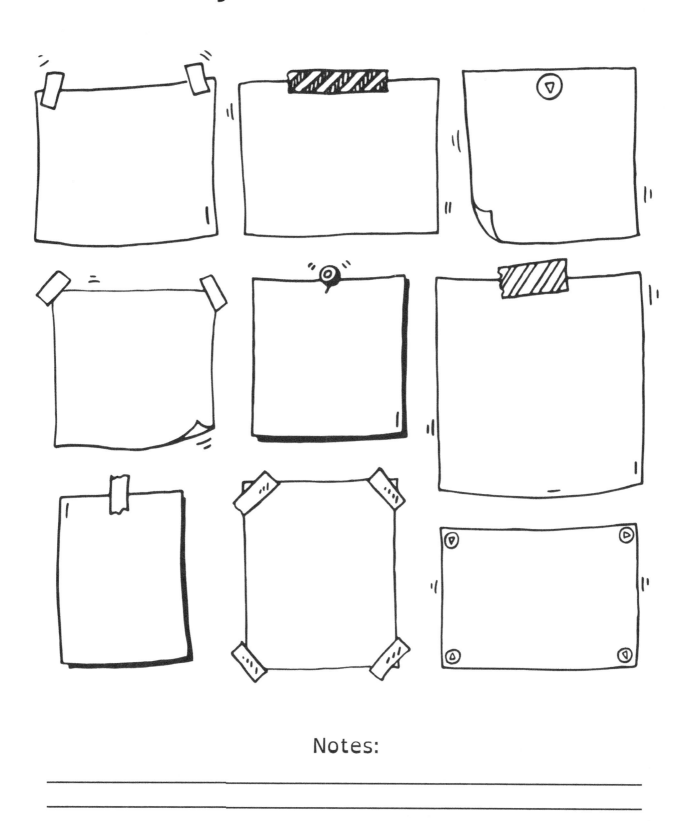

Notes:

_____

_____

_____

Nature Study

Go outside and make a realistic drawing of something you find in nature.

Reading Time - 1 Hour (Set a timer)

Choose Four Books - Read from each book for 15 minutes.

Copy important words or pictures from each book here:

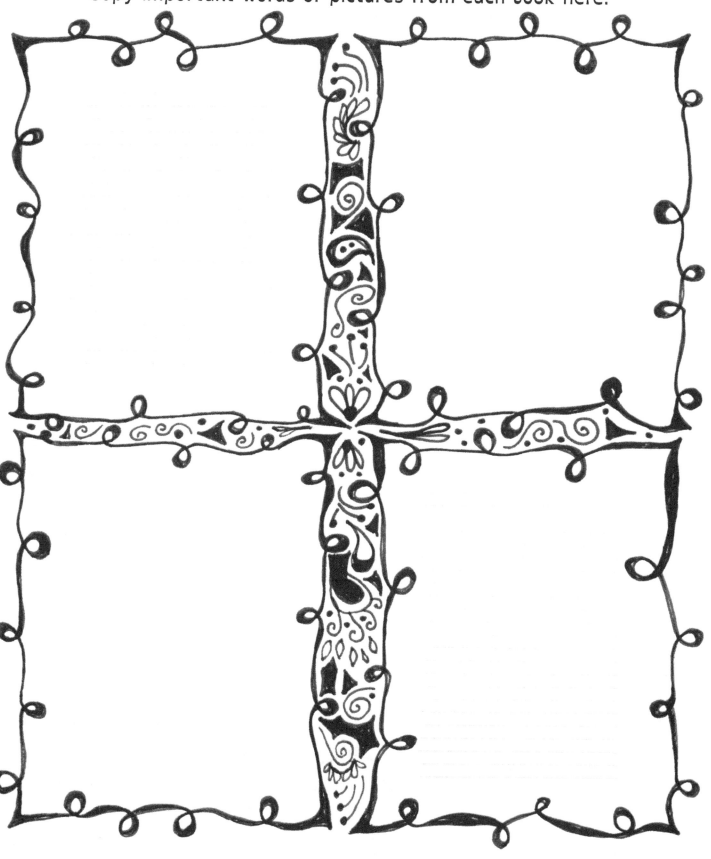

Spelling Time

Find 20 Words with **8** letters each.
Look around your house and in your
books for words. Write the words here:

_____   _____

_____   _____

_____   _____

_____   _____

_____   _____

_____   _____

_____   _____

_____   _____

_____   _____

_____   _____

Start Time:

Stop Time:

Screen Time!

Watch a Documentary, Educational Program, Movie, or Tutorial.

TITLE: _____

SUBJECT_____

LOCATION:_____

MESSAGE: _____

Rating:

AWFUL

BAD

LAME

YUCKY

OKAY

NICE

GOOD

GREAT

SUPER

Notes:

TITLE:

Draw a Scene from the video:

Use THIS PAGE for Math Practice

Or be creative and design something, like a house! You could make graphs, maps or geometric designs with this graph paper.

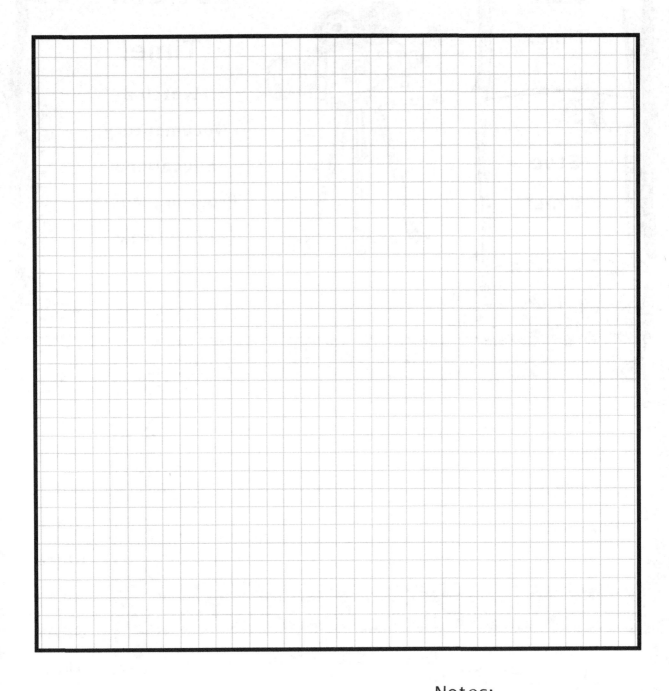

Notes:

_____

_____

_____

_____

Listening Time

Listen to an audio book or classical music or
ask someone to read a story to you while
you color and draw on the next page.

What are you listening to?

_____

Thinking Time!

Can you complete the puzzle?

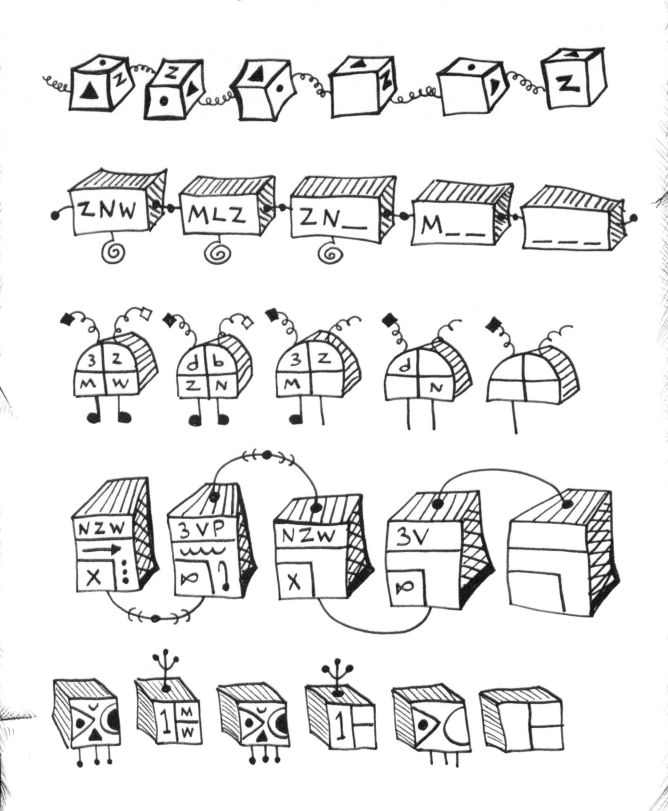

Travel Dreams Geography

Choose any City, any State or any Country:

Where would you like to go?

How far would you travel?

What would you pack?

----

what would you see?

What would you eat?

What is the weather like?

What makes this place unique?

Share an interesting fact:

Draw something you would see in this place:

Priority and Planning

Date:_____

A Quote

_____

_____

_____

To-Do List

_____

_____

_____

_____

My Plans

_____

_____

_____

My Goals

_____

_____

_____

Notes:

_____

_____

_____

_____

_____

Relax and be Creative

Practice working with your colored pencils.

Object Lesson

Look at this picture.

List four things that you understand about the object.

1._____

2._____

3._____

4._____

Journal

A Day in My Life

Nature Study

Go outside and make a realistic drawing of
something you find in nature.

Reading Time - 1 Hour (Set a timer)

Choose Four Books - Read from each book for 15 minutes.

Copy important words or pictures from each book here:

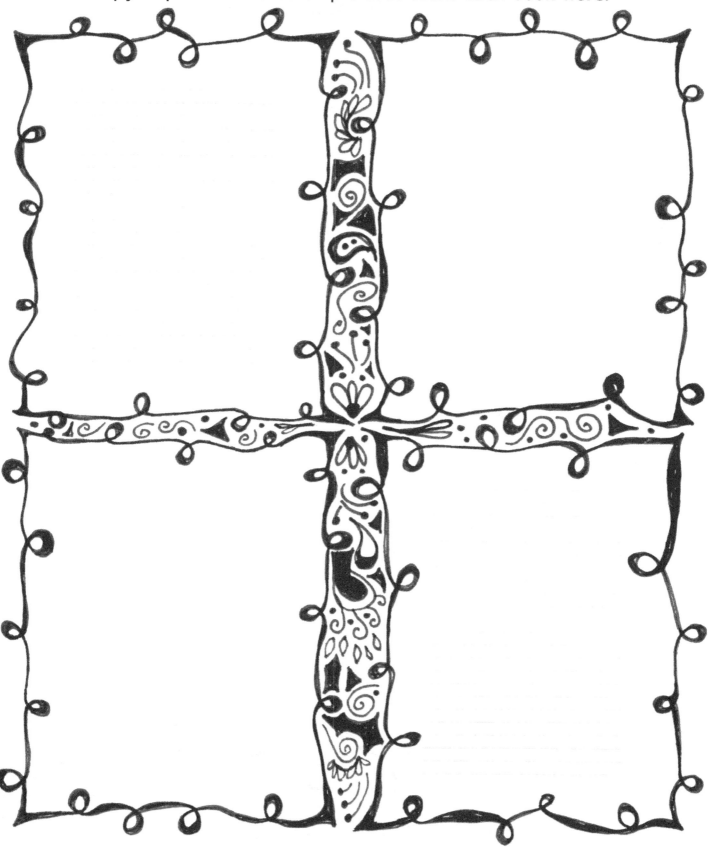

Spelling Time

Find 20 Words with **9** letters each.
Look around your house and in your
books for words. Write the words here:

_____   _____

_____   _____

_____   _____

_____   _____

_____   _____

_____   _____

_____   _____

_____   _____

_____   _____

_____   _____

Screen Time!

Start Time:

Stop Time:

Watch a Documentary, Educational Program, Movie, or Tutorial.

TITLE: _____

SUBJECT _____

LOCATION: _____

MESSAGE: _____

Rating:

AWFUL

BAD

LAME

YUCKY

OKAY

NICE

GOOD

GREAT

SUPER

Draw a Scene from the video:

Notes:

TITLE:

Use THIS PAGE for Math Practice

Or be creative and design something, like a house! You could make graphs, maps or geometric designs with this graph paper.

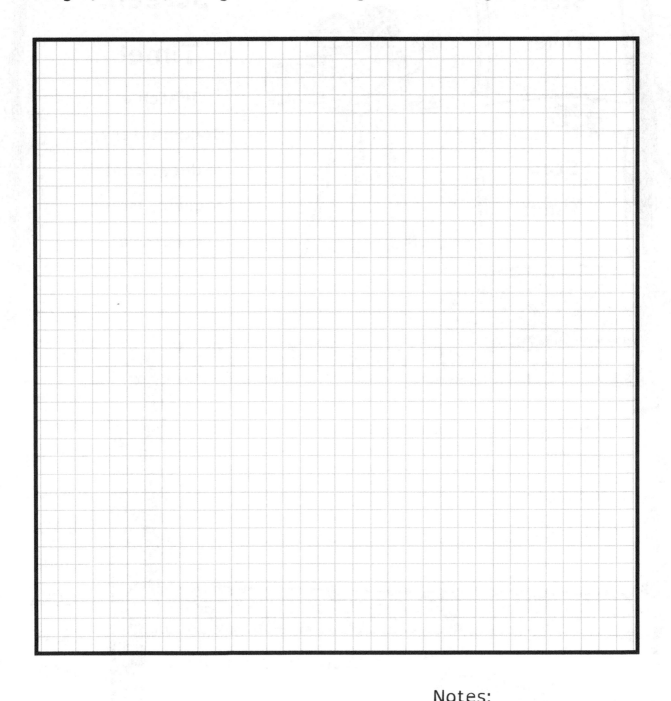

Notes:

_____

_____

_____

_____

World News Today!

Talk to your parents about current events.

Look at a newspaper, news broadcast or website.

Color the countries your learn about.

Tell the news stories with words or pictures.

Book of the Day

Choose a book from your stack that you want to focus on today.

Write and Draw to show what your are learning.

TITLE:_____

Thinking Time!

Can you complete the puzzle?

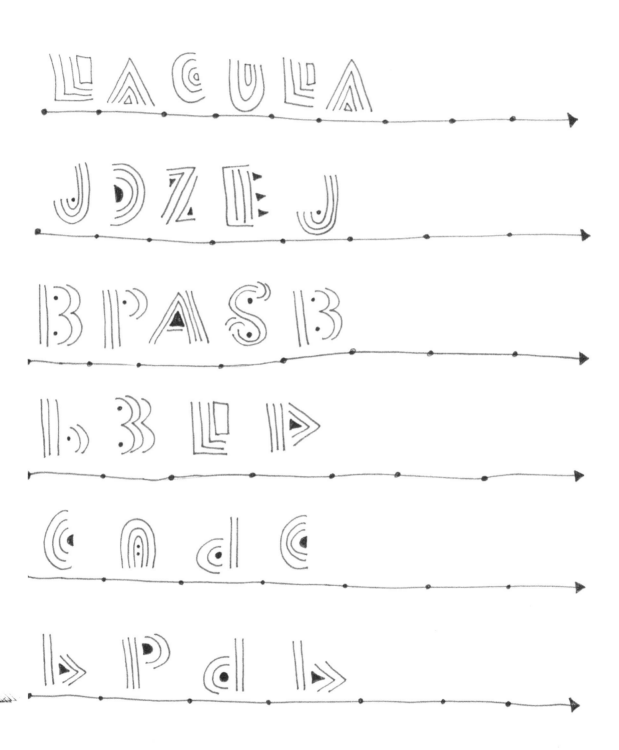

Travel Dreams Geography

Choose any City, any State or any Country:

Where would you like to go?

How far would you travel?

What would you pack?

----

what would you see?

What would you eat?

What is the weather like?

What makes this place unique?

Share an interesting fact:

Draw something you would see in this place:

Priority and Planning

Date:_____

A Quote
_____
_____
_____

To-Do List
_____
_____
_____

My Plans
_____
_____
_____

My Goals
_____
_____
_____

Notes:
_____
_____
_____
_____

Relax and be Creative

Practice working with your colored pencils.

Object Lesson

Look at this picture.

List four things that you understand about the object.

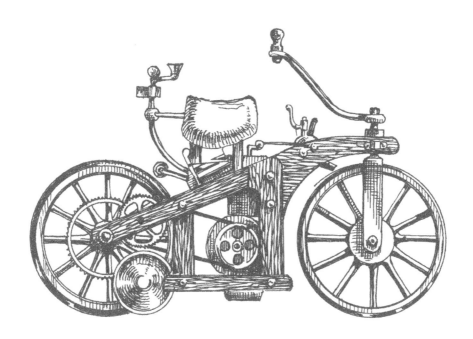

1._____

2._____

3._____

4._____

Just be Creative.

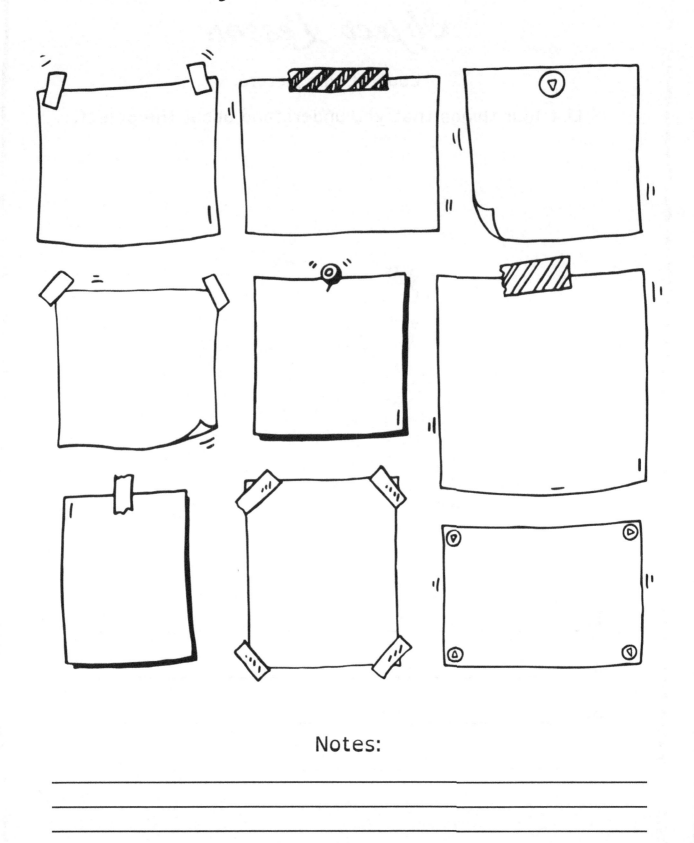

Notes:

_____
_____
_____

Start Time: _____

Stop Time:

Screen Time!

Watch a Documentary, Educational Program, Movie, or Tutorial.

TITLE: _____

SUBJECT _____

LOCATION: _____

MESSAGE: _____

Rating:

AWFUL

BAD

LAME

YUCKY

OKAY

NICE

GOOD

GREAT

SUPER

Notes:

TITLE:

Draw a Scene from the video:

Use THIS PAGE for Math Practice

Or be creative and design something, like a house! You could make graphs, maps or geometric designs with this graph paper.

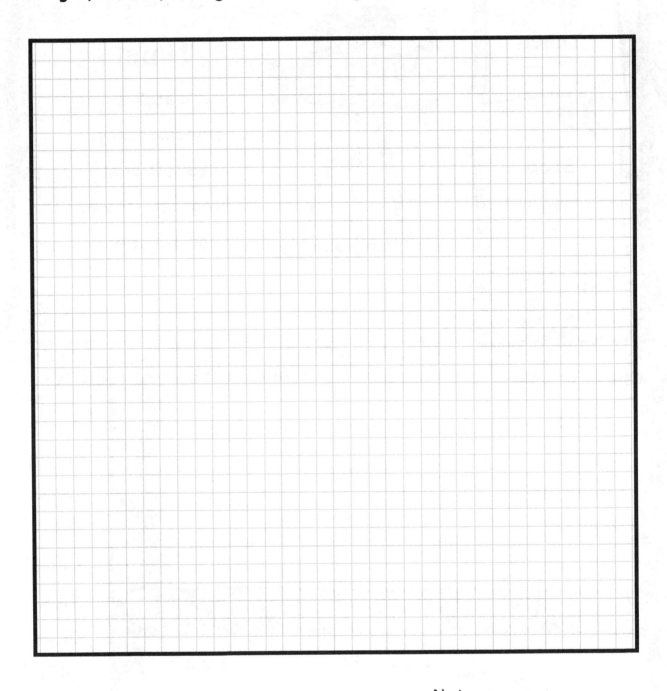

Notes:

_____

_____

_____

_____

Book of the Day

Choose a book from your stack that you want to focus on today.

Write and Draw to show what your are learning.

TITLE:_____

Travel Dreams Geography

Choose any City, any State or any Country:

Where would you like to go?

How far would you travel?

What would you pack?

----

what would you see?

What would you eat?

What is the weather like?

What makes this place unique?

Share an interesting fact:

Draw something you would see in this place:

Priority and Planning

Date:_____

A Quote

_____
_____
_____

To-Do List

_____
_____
_____
_____

My Plans

_____
_____
_____

My Goals

_____
_____
_____

Notes:

_____
_____
_____
_____

Relax and be Creative

Practice working with your colored pencils.

Object Lesson

Look at this picture.

List four things that you understand about the object.

1._____

2._____

3._____

4._____

Just be Creative.

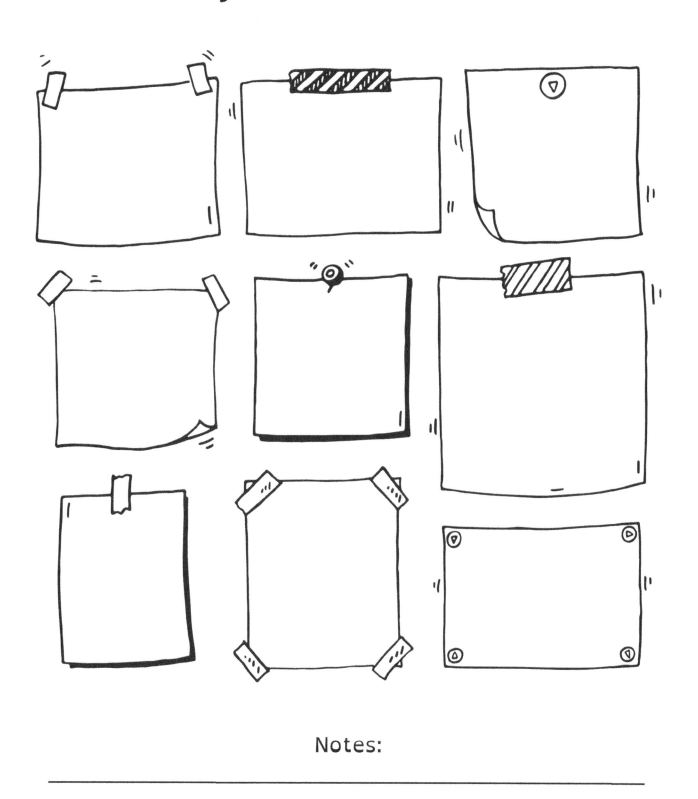

Notes:

_____

_____

_____

Nature Study

Go outside and make a realistic drawing of
something you find in nature.

Reading Time - 1 Hour (Set a timer)

Choose Four Books - Read from each book for 15 minutes.

Copy important words or pictures from each book here:

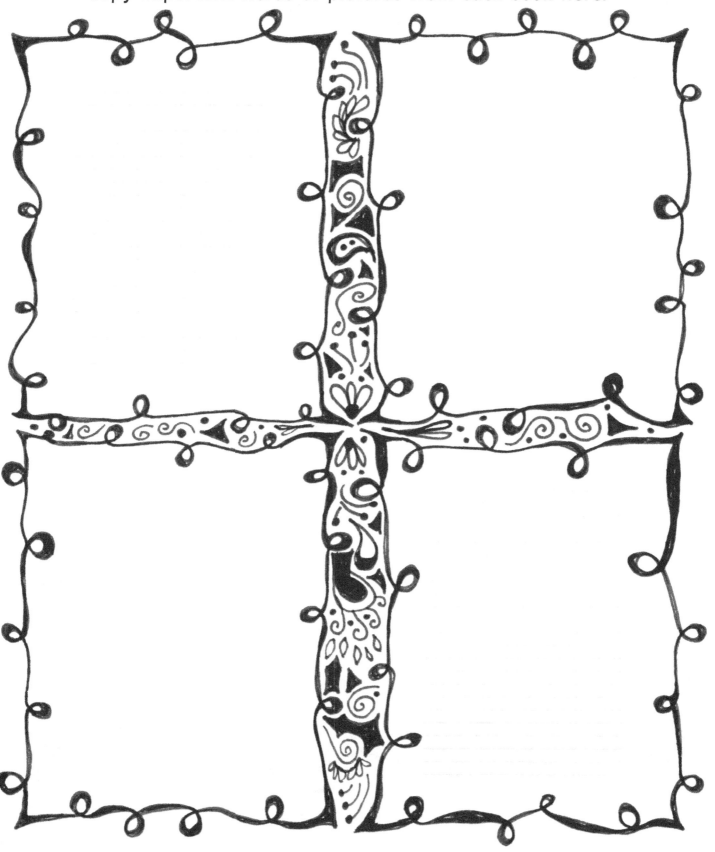

Spelling Time

Find 20 Words with 8 letters each.
Look around your house and in your
books for words. Write the words here:

Start Time:

Stop Time:

Screen Time!

Watch a Documentary, Educational Program, Movie, or Tutorial.

TITLE: _____

SUBJECT _____

LOCATION: _____

MESSAGE: _____

Rating:

AWFUL

BAD

LAME

YUCKY

OKAY

NICE

GOOD

GREAT

SUPER

Draw a Scene from the video:

Notes:

TITLE:

Book of the Day

Choose a book from your stack that you want to focus on today.

Write and Draw to show what your are learning.

TITLE:_____

Thinking Time!

Can you complete the puzzle?

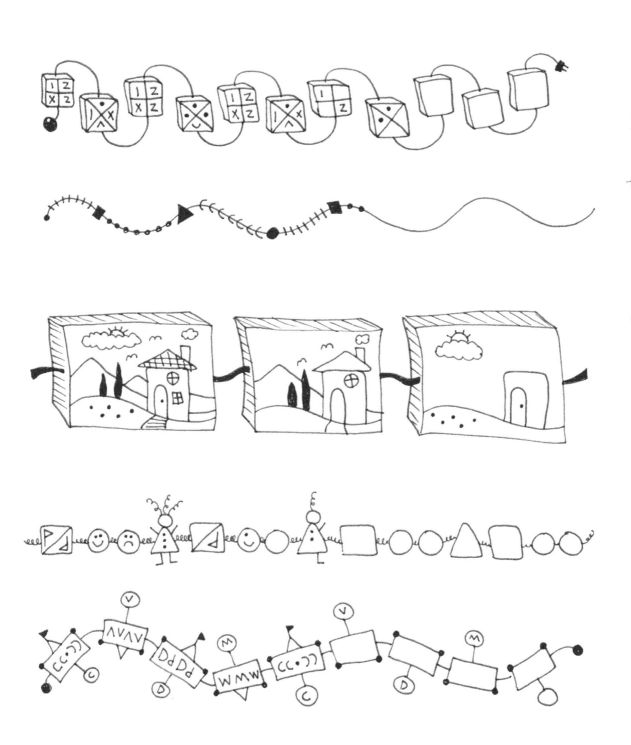

Travel Dreams Geography

Choose any City, any State or any Country:

Where would you like to go?

_____

How far would you travel?

_____

What would you pack?

_____

what would you see?

_____

What would you eat?

_____

What is the weather like?

_____

What makes this place unique?

_____

Share an interesting fact:

_____

Draw something you would see in this place:

Priority and Planning

Date:_____

A Quote

_____
_____
_____

To-Do List

_____
_____
_____
_____

My Plans

_____
_____
_____
_____

My Goals

_____
_____
_____

Notes:

_____
_____
_____
_____
_____

Object Lesson

Look at this picture.

List four things that you understand about the object.

1._____

2._____

3._____

4._____

Nature Study

Go outside and make a realistic drawing of something you find in nature.

Reading Time - 1 Hour (Set a timer)

Choose Four Books - Read from each book for 15 minutes.

Copy important words or pictures from each book here:

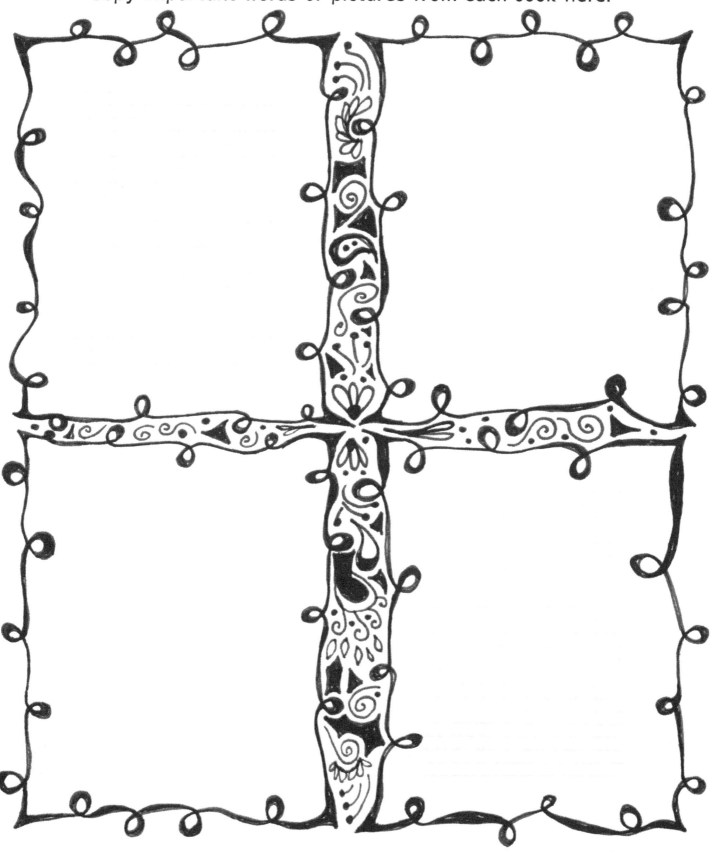

Spelling Time

Find 20 Words with **7** letters each.
Look around your house and in your
books for words. Write the words here:

_____   _____

_____   _____

_____   _____

_____   _____

_____   _____

_____   _____

_____   _____

_____   _____

_____   _____

_____   _____

Start Time: _____

Stop Time:

Screen Time!

Watch a Documentary, Educational Program, Movie, or Tutorial.

TITLE: _____

SUBJECT _____

LOCATION: _____

MESSAGE: _____

Rating:

AWFUL

BAD

LAME

YUCKY

OKAY

NICE

GOOD

GREAT

SUPER

Notes:

TITLE:

Draw a Scene from the video:

Use THIS PAGE for Math Practice

Or be creative and design something, like a house! You could make graphs, maps or geometric designs with this graph paper.

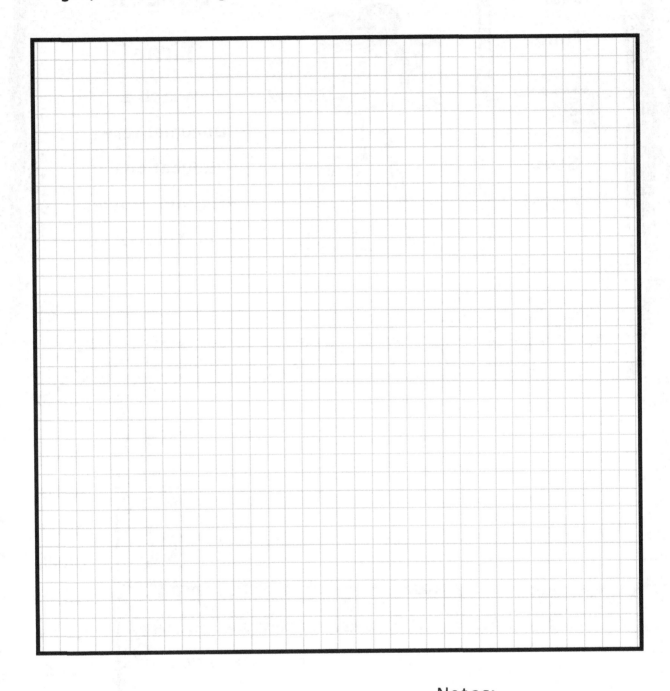

Notes:

_____

_____

_____

_____

Font Writing Practice:

ABCDEFGHIJKLMNOPQRSTUVWXYZ

abcdefghijklmnopqrstuvwxyz

ABCDEFGHIJKLMNOPQRSTUVWXYZ

ABCDEFGHIJKLMNOPQRSTUVWXYZ

Abcdefghijklmnopqrstuvwxyz

Develop Your Own Style

Book of the Day

Choose a book from your stack that you want to focus on today.

Write and Draw to show what your are learning.

TITLE:_____

Travel Dreams Geography

Choose any City, any State or any Country:

Where would you like to go?

How far would you travel?

What would you pack?

----

what would you see?

What would you eat?

What is the weather like?

What makes this place unique?

Share an interesting fact:

Draw something you would see in this place:

Priority and Planning

Date:_____

A Quote
_____
_____
_____
_____

To-Do List
_____
_____
_____
_____

My Plans
_____
_____
_____

My Goals
_____
_____
_____

Notes:
_____
_____
_____
_____

Relax and be Creative

Practice working with your colored pencils.

Object Lesson

Look at this picture.

List four things that you understand about the object.

1. _____

2. _____

3. _____

4. _____

Journal

A Day in My Life

Nature Study

Go outside and make a realistic drawing of something you find in nature.

Reading Time - 1 Hour (Set a timer)

Choose Four Books - Read from each book for 15 minutes.

Copy important words or pictures from each book here:

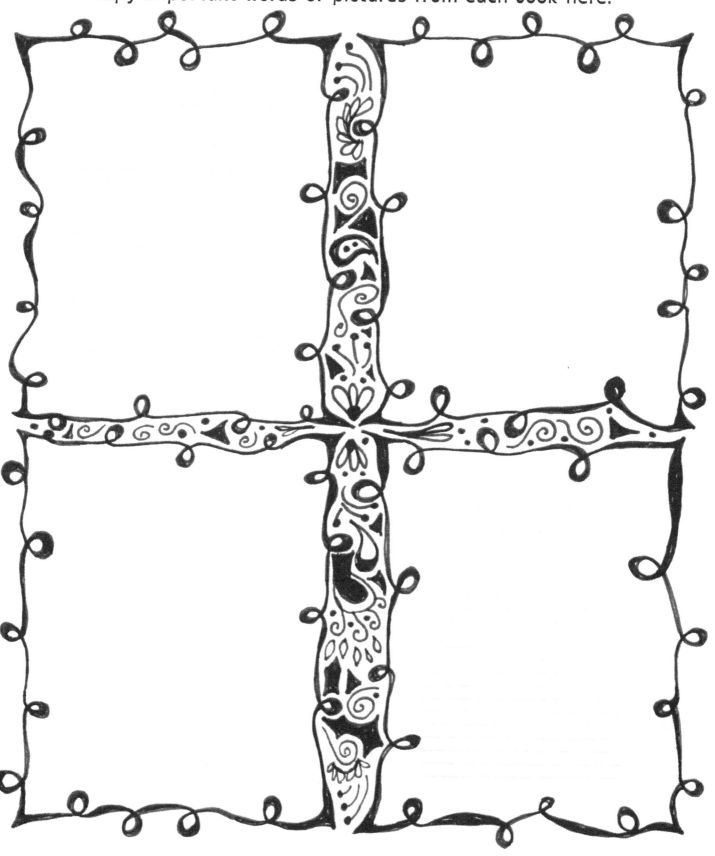

Spelling Time

6

Find 20 Words with ___ letters each.
Look around your house and in your
books for words. Write the words here:

Start Time:

Stop Time:

Screen Time!

Watch a Documentary, Educational Program, Movie, or Tutorial.

TITLE: _____

SUBJECT _____

LOCATION: _____

MESSAGE: _____

Rating:

AWFUL

BAD

LAME

YUCKY

OKAY

NICE

GOOD

GREAT

SUPER

Notes:

TITLE:

Draw a Scene from the video:

Use THIS PAGE for Math Practice

Or be creative and design something, like a house! You could make graphs, maps or geometric designs with this graph paper.

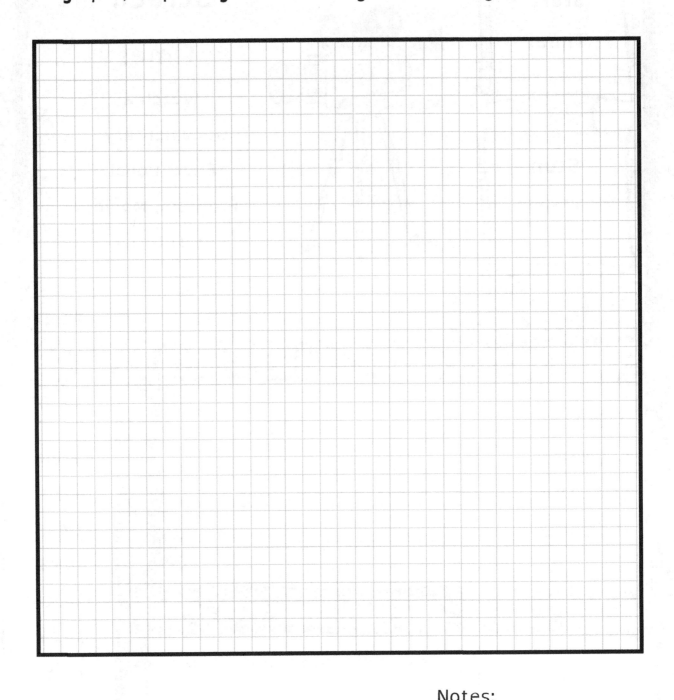

Notes:

_____

_____

_____

_____

Book of the Day

Choose a book from your stack that you want to focus on today.

Write and Draw to show what your are learning.

TITLE:_____

Thinking Time!

Can you complete the puzzle?

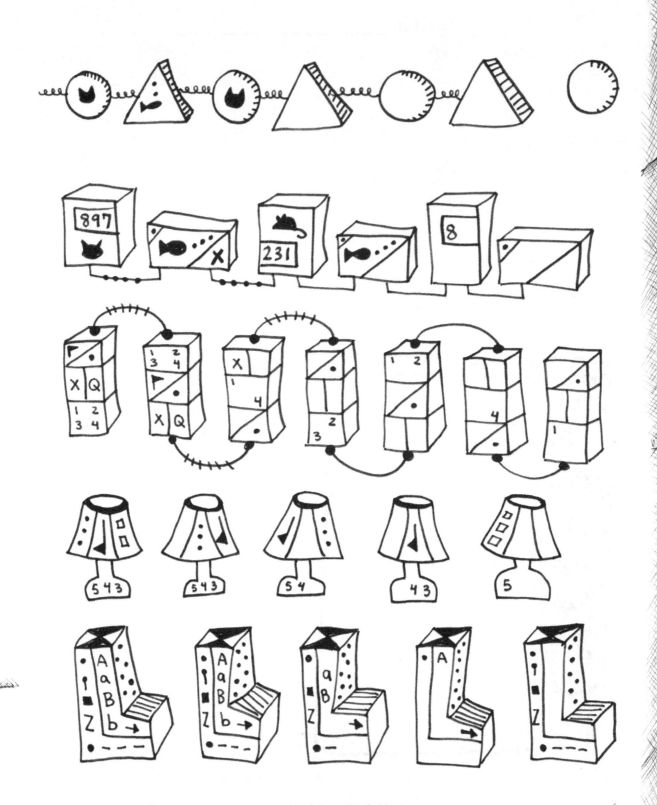

Travel Dreams Geography

Choose any City, any State or any Country:

Where would you like to go?

How far would you travel?

What would you pack?

----

what would you see?

What would you eat?

What is the weather like?

What makes this place unique?

Share an interesting fact:

Draw something you would see in this place:

Priority and Planning

Date:_____

A Quote
_____
_____
_____

To-Do List
_____
_____
_____
_____

My Plans
_____
_____
_____

My Goals
_____
_____
_____

Notes:
_____
_____
_____
_____

Relax and be Creative

Practice working with your colored pencils.

Object Lesson

Look at this picture.

List four things that you understand about the object.

1. _____

2. _____

3. _____

4. _____

Just be Creative.

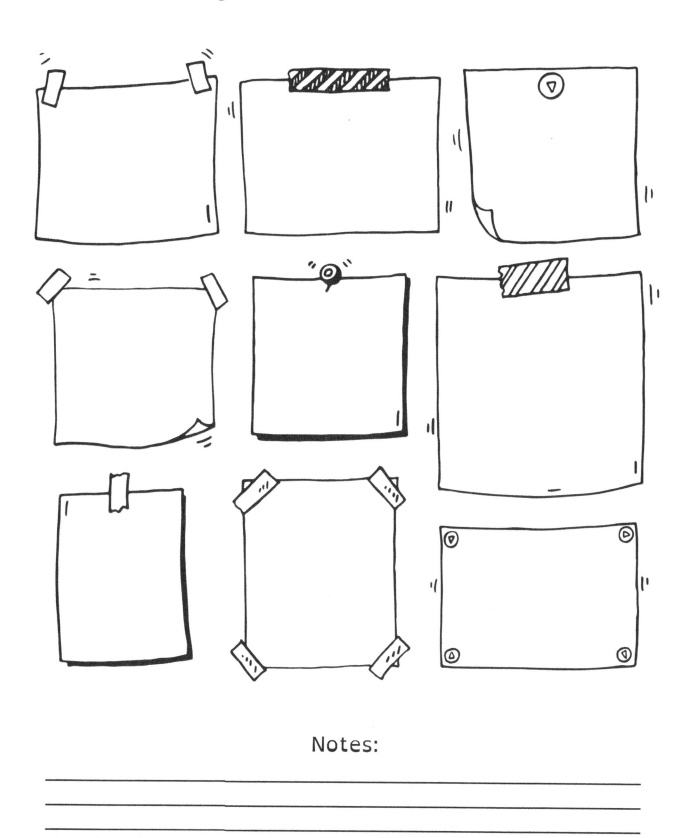

Notes:

_____

_____

_____

Nature Study

Go outside and make a realistic drawing of
something you find in nature.

Reading Time - 1 Hour (Set a timer)

Choose Four Books - Read from each book for 15 minutes.

Copy important words or pictures from each book here:

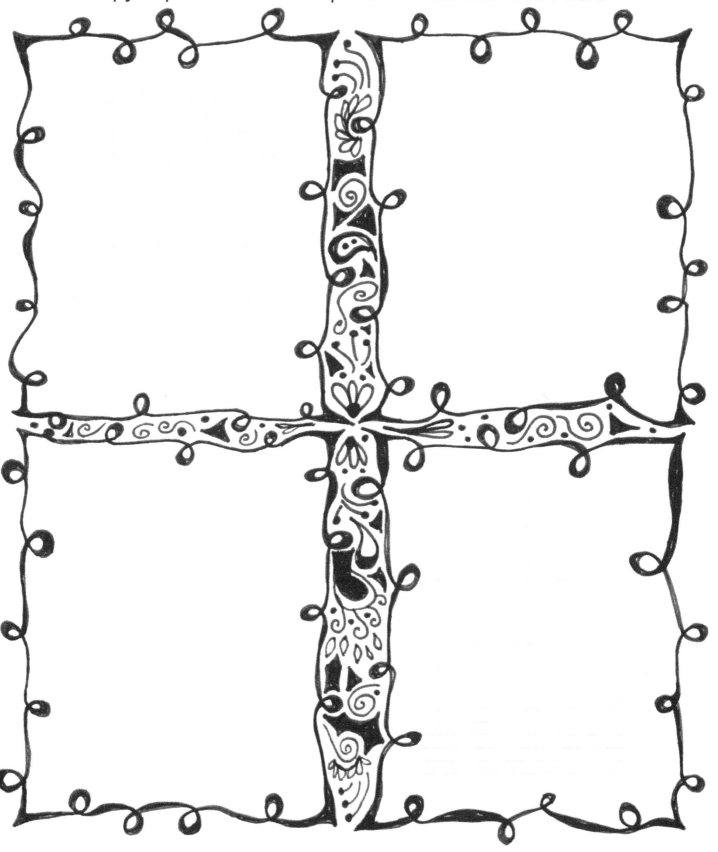

Spelling Time

5

Find 20 Words with ____ letters each.
Look around your house and in your
books for words. Write the words here:

_____   _____

_____   _____

_____   _____

_____   _____

_____   _____

_____   _____

_____   _____

_____   _____

_____   _____

_____   _____

Screen Time!

Start Time:

Stop Time:

Watch a Documentary, Educational Program, Movie, or Tutorial.

TITLE: _____

SUBJECT_____

LOCATION:_____

MESSAGE: _____

Rating:

AWFUL

BAD

LAME

YUCKY

OKAY

NICE

GOOD

GREAT

SUPER

Notes:

Draw a Scene from the video:

TITLE:

Use THIS PAGE for Math Practice

Or be creative and design something, like a house! You could make graphs, maps or geometric designs with this graph paper.

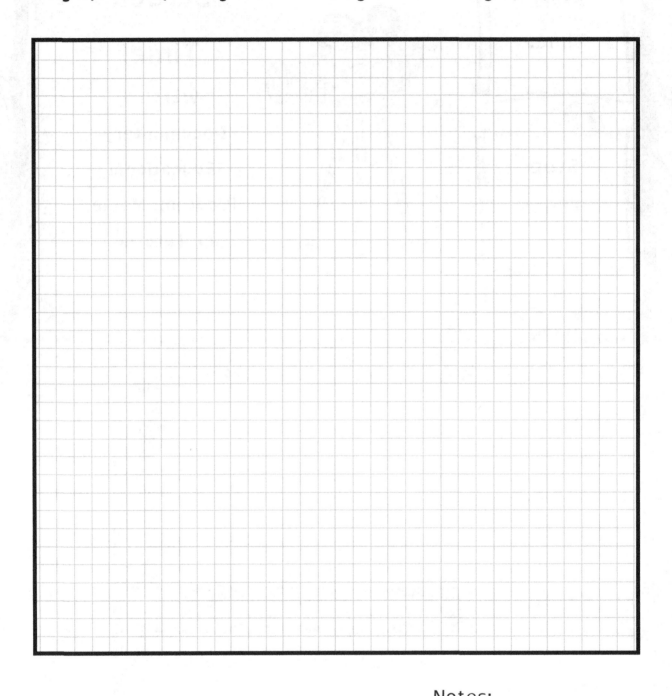

Notes:

_____
_____
_____
_____

World News Today!

Talk to your parents about current events.

Look at a newspaper, news broadcast or website.

Color the countries your learn about.

Tell the news stories with words or pictures.

Book of the Day

Choose a book from your stack that you want to focus on today.

Write and Draw to show what your are learning.

TITLE:_____

Thinking Time!

Can you complete the puzzle?

Travel Dreams Geography

Choose any City, any State or any Country:

Where would you like to go?

How far would you travel?

What would you pack?

----

what would you see?

What would you eat?

What is the weather like?

What makes this place unique?

Share an interesting fact:

Draw something you would see in this place:

Priority and Planning

Date:_____

A Quote
_____
_____
_____
_____

To-Do List
_____
_____
_____
_____
_____

My Plans
_____
_____
_____
_____

My Goals
_____
_____
_____
_____

Notes:
_____
_____
_____
_____
_____

Relax and be Creative

Practice working with your colored pencils.

Object Lesson

Look at this picture.

List four things that you understand about the object.

1._____

2._____

3._____

4._____

Nature Study

Go outside and make a realistic drawing of
something you find in nature.

Reading Time - 1 Hour (Set a timer)

Choose Four Books - Read from each book for 15 minutes.

Copy important words or pictures from each book here:

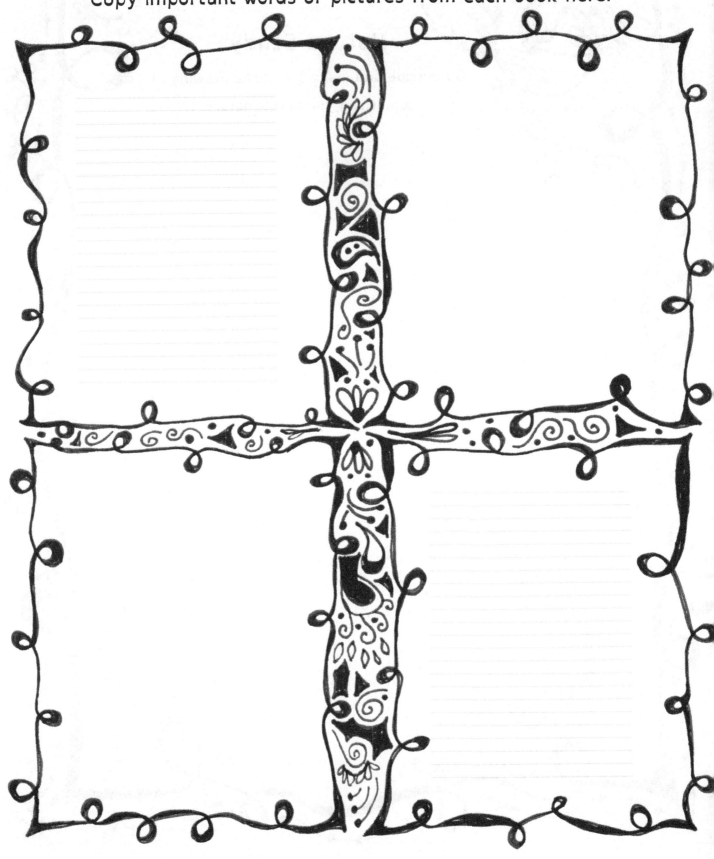

Spelling Time

6

Find 20 Words with   letters each.
Look around your house and in your books for words. Write the words here:

Start Time: _____

Stop Time:

Screen Time!

Watch a Documentary, Educational Program, Movie, or Tutorial.

TITLE: _____

SUBJECT _____

LOCATION: _____

MESSAGE: _____

Rating:

AWFUL

BAD

LAME

YUCKY

OKAY

NICE

GOOD

GREAT

SUPER

Notes:

TITLE:

Draw a Scene from the video:

Use THIS PAGE for Math Practice

Or be creative and design something, like a house! You could make graphs, maps or geometric designs with this graph paper.

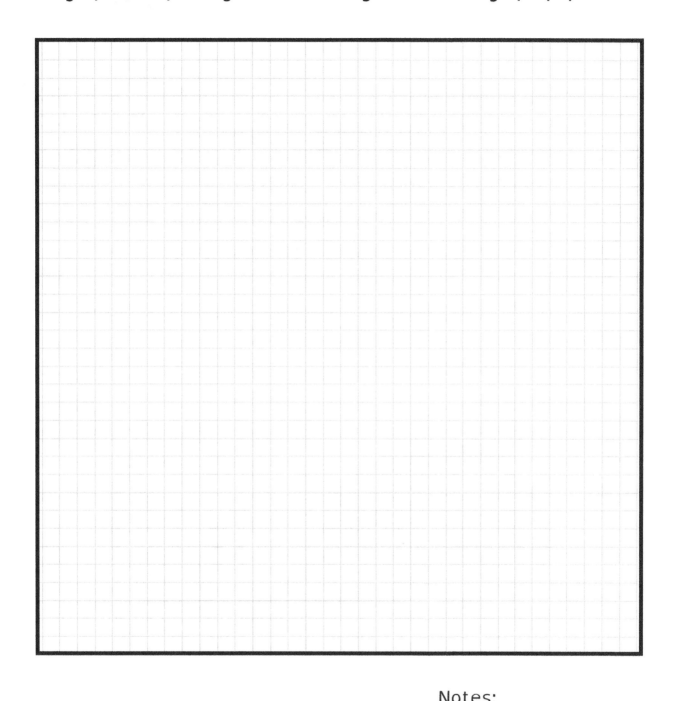

Notes:

_____

_____

_____

_____

Listening Time

Listen to an audio book or classical music or ask someone to read a story to you while you color and draw on the next page.

What are you listening to?

_____

Thinking Time!

Can you complete the puzzle?

Travel Dreams Geography

Choose any City, any State or any Country:

Where would you like to go?

How far would you travel?

What would you pack?

----

what would you see?

What would you eat?

What is the weather like?

What makes this place unique?

Share an interesting fact:

Draw something you would see in this place:

Priority and Planning

Date:_____

A Quote

_____
_____
_____

To-Do List

_____
_____
_____

My Plans

_____
_____
_____

My Goals

_____
_____
_____

Notes:

_____
_____
_____
_____
_____

Object Lesson

Look at this picture.

List four things that you understand about the object.

1._____

2._____

3._____

4._____

Just be Creative.

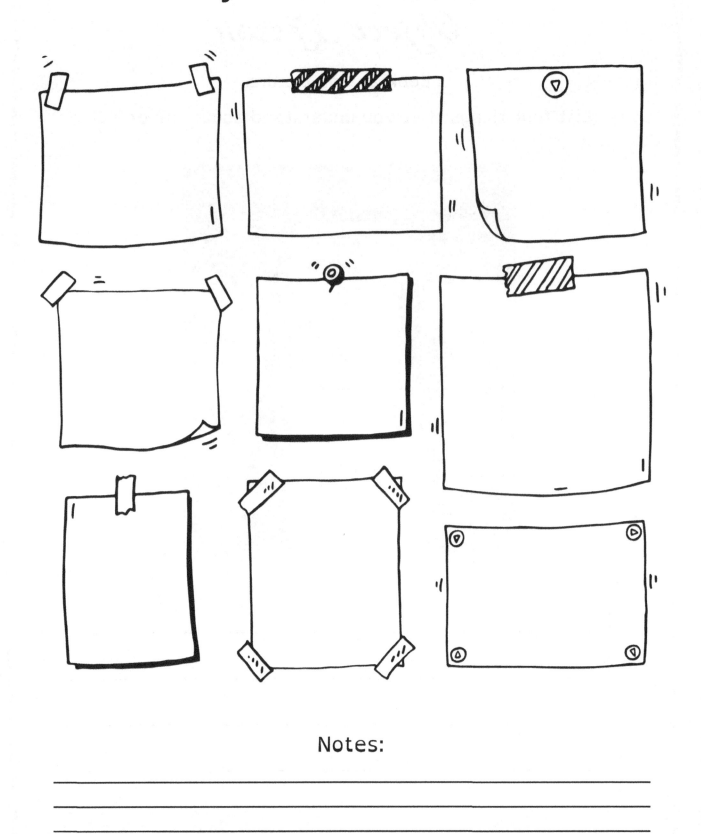

Notes:
_____
_____
_____

Nature Study

Go outside and make a realistic drawing of something you find in nature.

Reading Time - 1 Hour (Set a timer)

Choose Four Books - Read from each book for 15 minutes.

Copy important words or pictures from each book here:

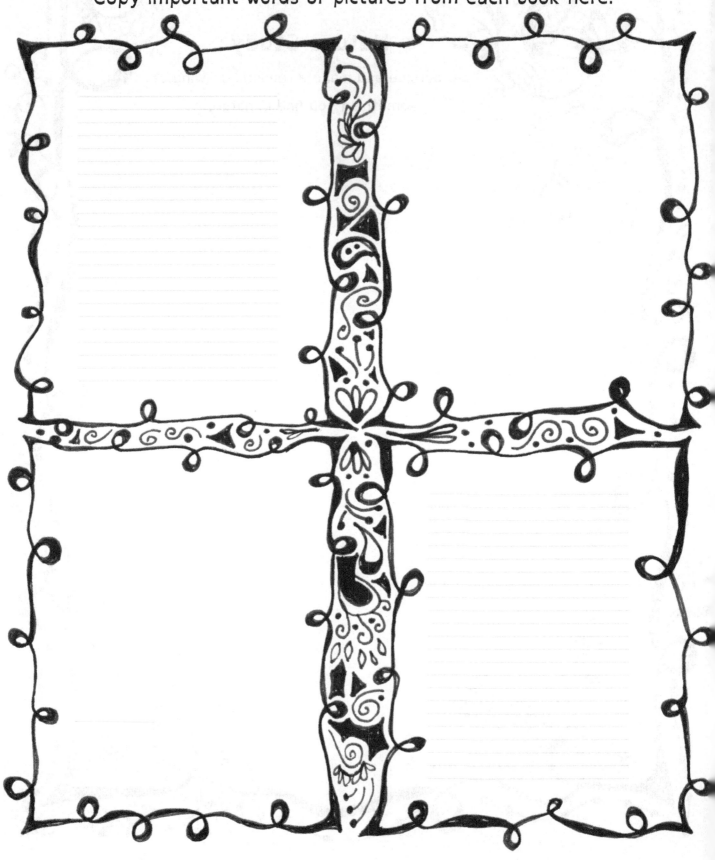

Spelling Time

Find 20 Words with 7 letters each.
Look around your house and in your
books for words. Write the words here:

_____   _____

_____   _____

_____   _____

_____   _____

_____   _____

_____   _____

_____   _____

_____   _____

_____   _____

_____   _____

Start Time:

Stop Time:

Screen Time!

Watch a Documentary, Educational Program, Movie, or Tutorial.

TITLE: _____

SUBJECT _____

LOCATION: _____

MESSAGE: _____

Rating:

AWFUL

BAD

LAME

YUCKY

OKAY

NICE

GOOD

GREAT

SUPER

Draw a Scene from the video:

Notes:

TITLE:

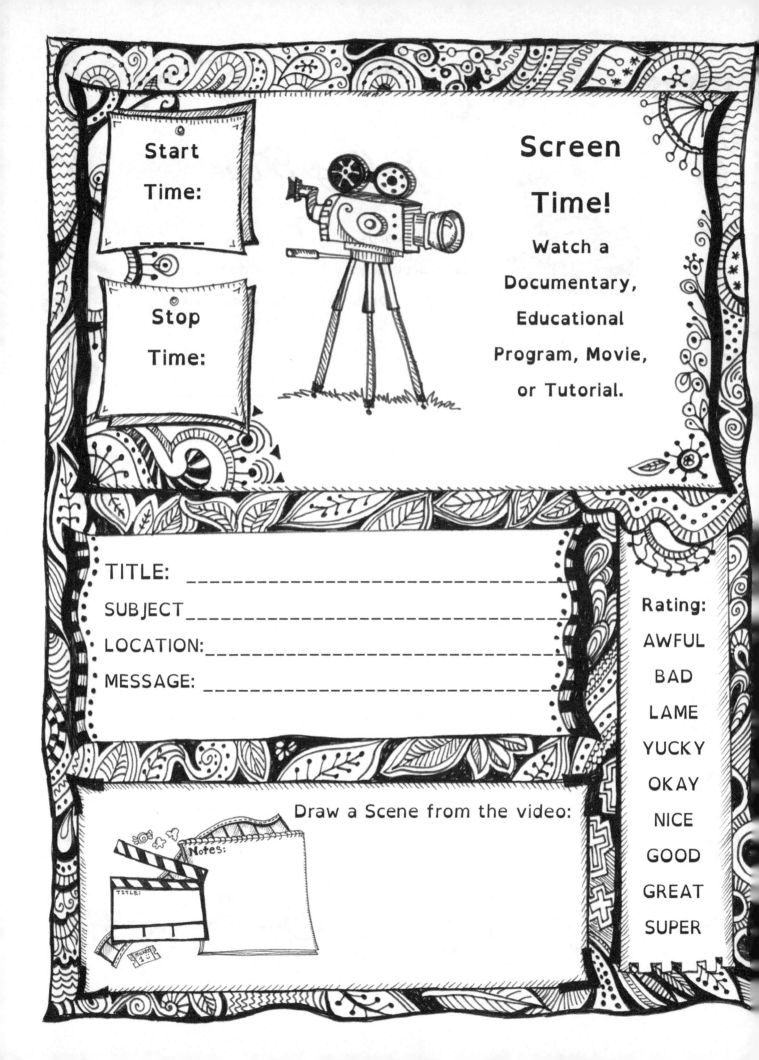

Use THIS PAGE for Math Practice

Or be creative and design something, like a house! You could make graphs, maps or geometric designs with this graph paper.

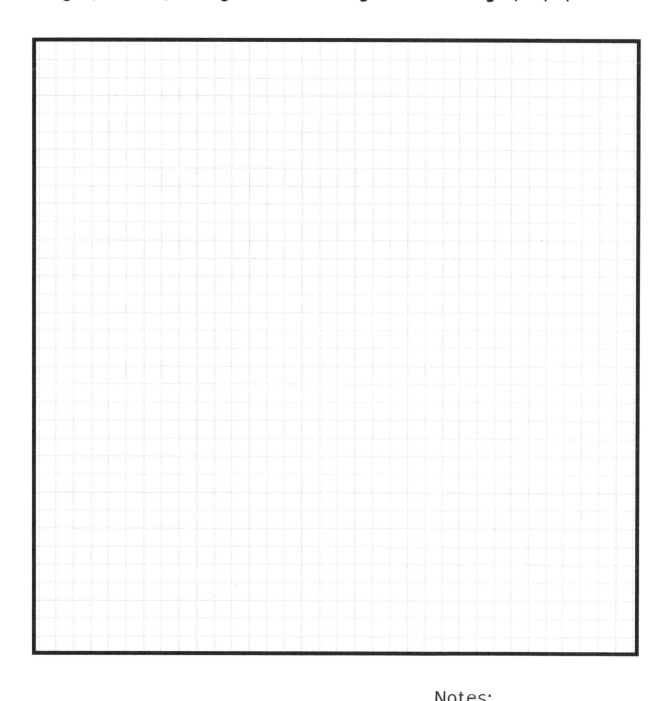

Notes:

_____

_____

_____

_____

Font Writing Practice:

ABCDEFGHIJKLMNOPQRSTUVWXYZ

abcdefghijklmnopqrstuvwxyz

ABCDEFGHIJKLMNOPQRSTUVWXYZ

ABCDEFGHIJKLMNOPQRSTUVWXYZ

Abcdefghijklmnopqrstuvwxyz

Develop Your Own Style

Book of the Day

Choose a book from your stack that you want to focus on today.

Write and Draw to show what your are learning.

TITLE:_____

Travel Dreams Geography

Choose any City, any State or any Country:

Where would you like to go?

How far would you travel?

What would you pack?

----

what would you see?

What would you eat?

What is the weather like?

What makes this place unique?

Share an interesting fact:

Draw something you would see in this place:

Priority and Planning

Date:_____

A Quote

_____

_____

_____

To-Do List

_____

_____

_____

_____

_____

My Plans

_____

_____

_____

My Goals

_____

_____

_____

Notes:

_____

_____

_____

_____

_____

Thinking Time!

Can you complete the puzzle?

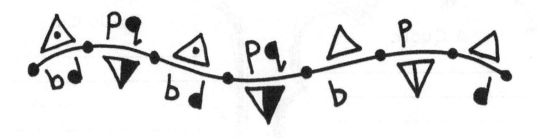

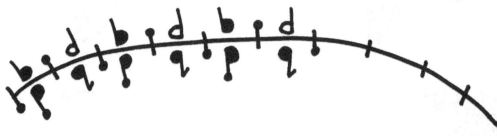

Object Lesson

Look at this picture.

List four things that you understand about the object.

1._____

2._____

3._____

4._____

Journal

A Day in My Life

Nature Study

Go outside and make a realistic drawing of something you find in nature.

Reading Time - 1 Hour (Set a timer)

Choose Four Books - Read from each book for 15 minutes.

Copy important words or pictures from each book here:

Spelling Time

Find 20 Words with **8** letters each.
Look around your house and in your
books for words. Write the words here:

Start Time: _____

Stop Time: _____

Screen Time!

Watch a Documentary, Educational Program, Movie, or Tutorial.

TITLE: _____

SUBJECT _____

LOCATION: _____

MESSAGE: _____

Rating:

AWFUL

BAD

LAME

YUCKY

OKAY

NICE

GOOD

GREAT

SUPER

Draw a Scene from the video:

Notes:

Use THIS PAGE for Math Practice

Or be creative and design something, like a house! You could make graphs, maps or geometric designs with this graph paper.

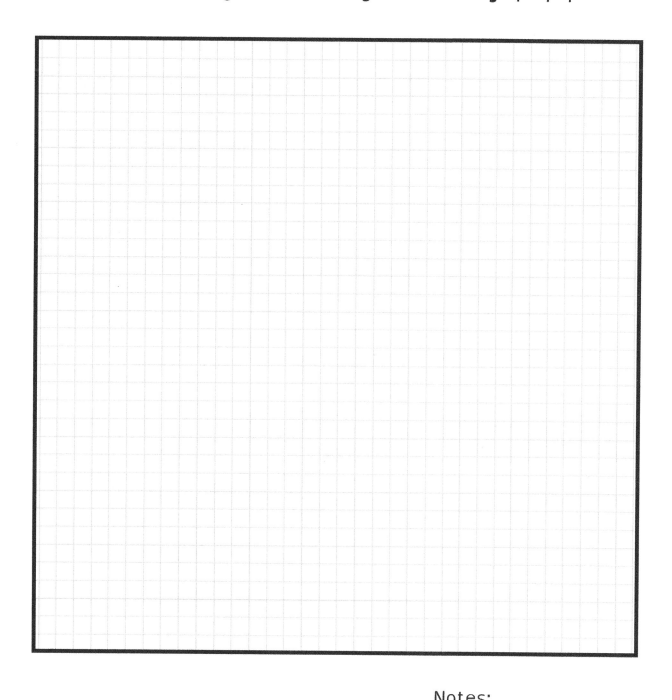

Notes:

_____

_____

_____

_____

Book of the Day

Choose a book from your stack that you want to focus on today.

Write and Draw to show what your are learning.

TITLE:_____

Thinking Time!

Can you complete the puzzle?

Travel Dreams Geography

Choose any City, any State or any Country:

Where would you like to go?

How far would you travel?

What would you pack?

----

what would you see?

What would you eat?

What is the weather like?

What makes this place unique?

Share an interesting fact:

Draw something you would see in this place:

Priority and Planning

Date:_____

A Quote

_____

_____

_____

_____

To-Do List

_____

_____

_____

_____

My Plans

_____

_____

_____

_____

My Goals

_____

_____

_____

_____

Notes:

_____

_____

_____

_____

_____

Object Lesson

Look at this picture.

List four things that you understand about the object.

1._____

2._____

3._____

4._____

Nature Study

Go outside and make a realistic drawing of
something you find in nature.

Reading Time - 1 Hour (Set a timer)

Choose Four Books - Read from each book for 15 minutes.

Copy important words or pictures from each book here:

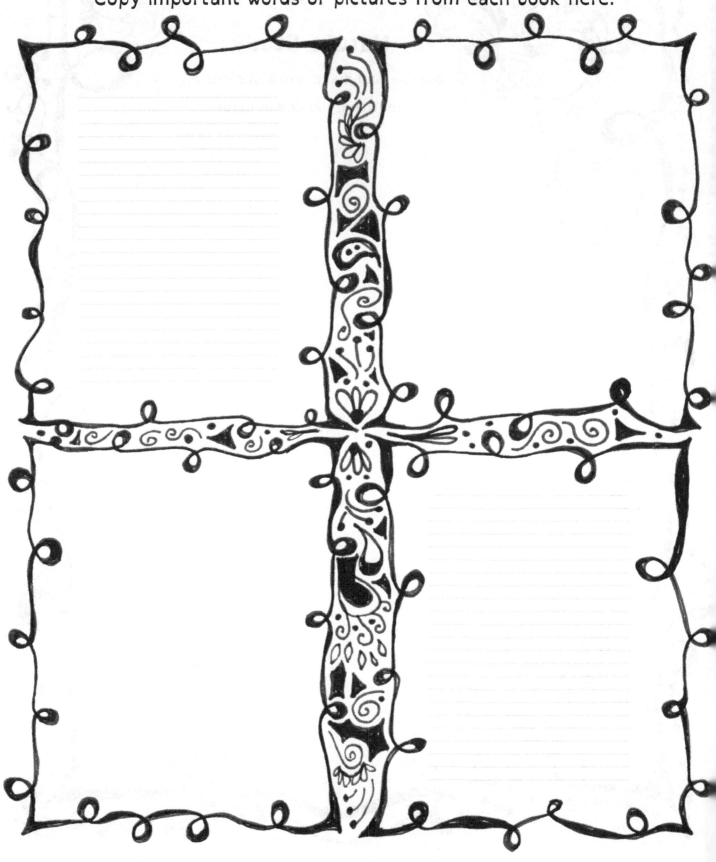

Spelling Time

Find 20 Words with 7 letters each.
Look around your house and in your
books for words. Write the words here:

Start Time:

Stop Time:

Screen Time!

Watch a Documentary, Educational Program, Movie, or Tutorial.

TITLE: _____

SUBJECT _____

LOCATION: _____

MESSAGE: _____

Rating:

AWFUL

BAD

LAME

YUCKY

OKAY

NICE

GOOD

GREAT

SUPER

Draw a Scene from the video:

Notes:

TITLE:

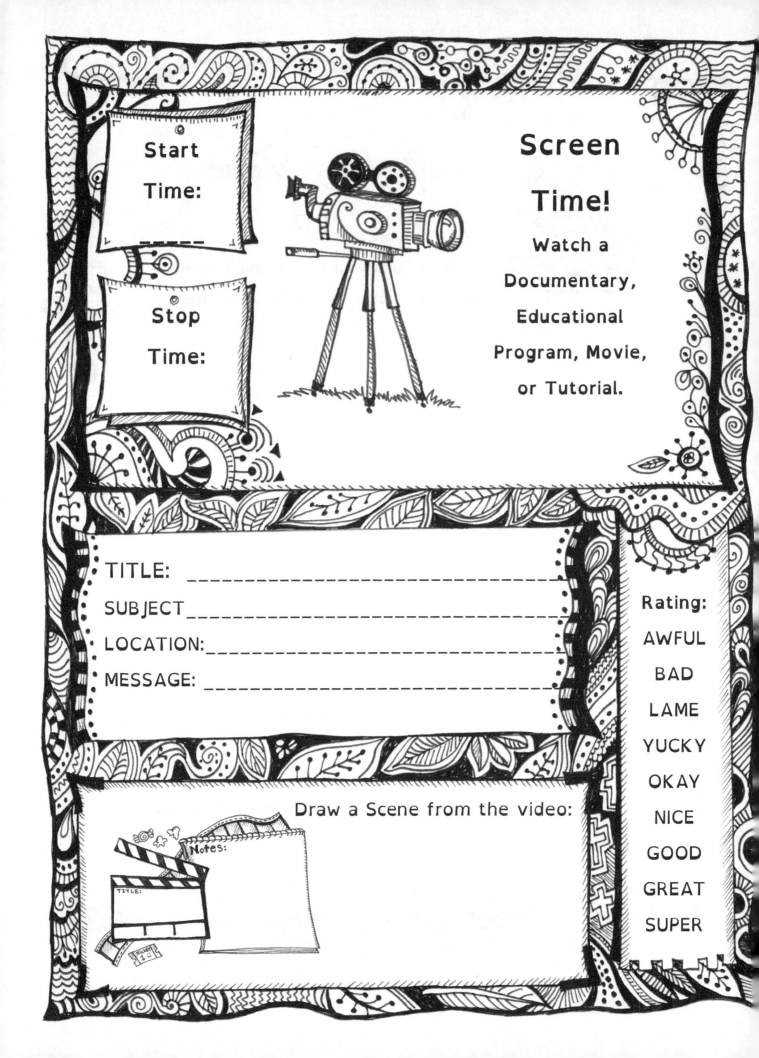

Use THIS PAGE for Math Practice

Or be creative and design something, like a house! You could make graphs, maps or geometric designs with this graph paper.

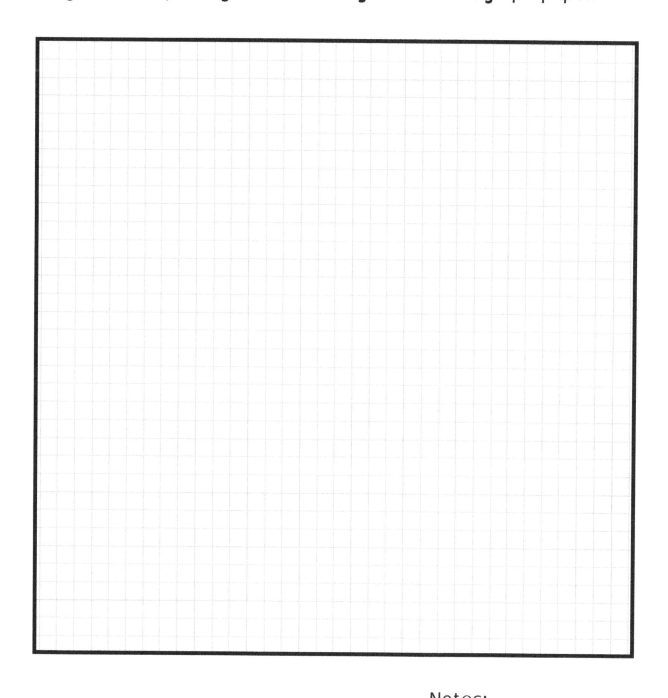

Notes:

_____

_____

_____

_____

Book of the Day

Choose a book from your stack that you want to focus on today.

Write and Draw to show what your are learning.

TITLE:_____

Thinking Time!

Can you complete the puzzle?

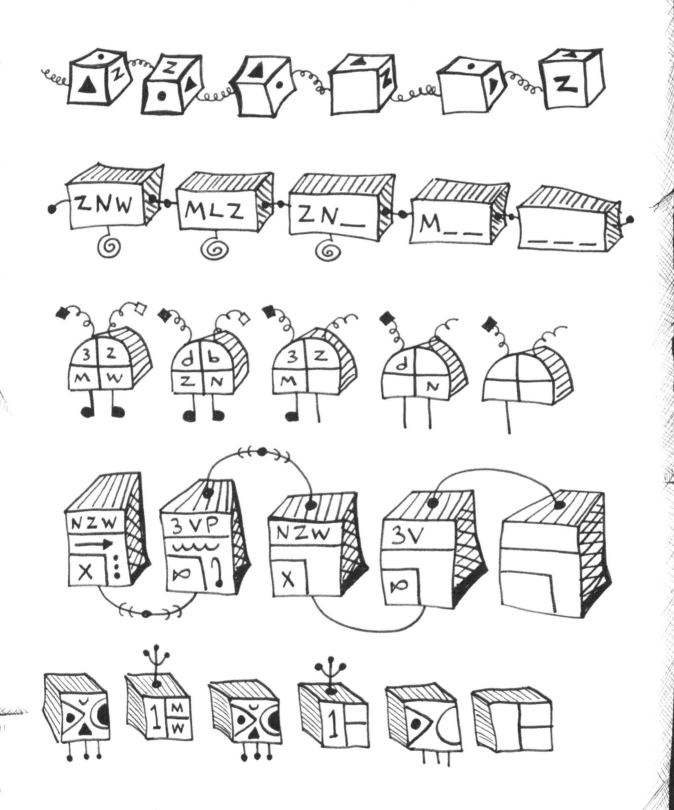

Travel Dreams Geography

Choose any City, any State or any Country:

Where would you like to go?

_____

How far would you travel?

_____

What would you pack?

_____

what would you see?

_____

What would you eat?

_____

What is the weather like?

_____

What makes this place unique?

_____

Share an interesting fact:

_____

Draw something you would see in this place:

Priority and Planning

Date:_____

A Quote

_____
_____
_____

To-Do List

_____
_____
_____
_____

My Plans

_____
_____
_____

My Goals

_____
_____
_____

Notes:

_____
_____
_____
_____
_____

Object Lesson

Look at this picture.

List four things that you understand about the object.

1._____

2._____

3._____

4._____

Nature Study

Go outside and make a realistic drawing of
something you find in nature.

Reading Time - 1 Hour (Set a timer)

Choose Four Books - Read from each book for 15 minutes.

Copy important words or pictures from each book here:

Spelling Time

Find 20 Words with **7** letters each.
Look around your house and in your
books for words. Write the words here:

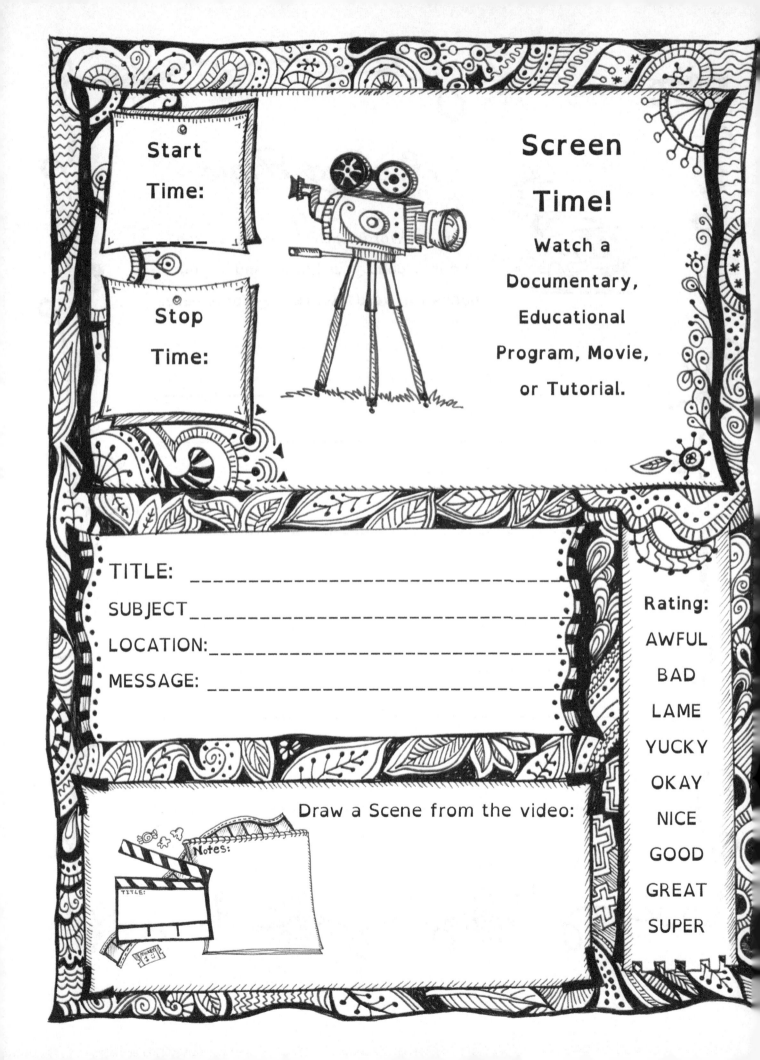

Start
Time:
_ _ _ _

Stop
Time:

Screen
Time!
Watch a
Documentary,
Educational
Program, Movie,
or Tutorial.

TITLE: _____

SUBJECT_____

LOCATION:_____

MESSAGE: _____

Rating:
AWFUL
BAD
LAME
YUCKY
OKAY
NICE
GOOD
GREAT
SUPER

Draw a Scene from the video:

Notes:

TITLE:

Use THIS PAGE for Math Practice

Or be creative and design something, like a house! You could make graphs, maps or geometric designs with this graph paper.

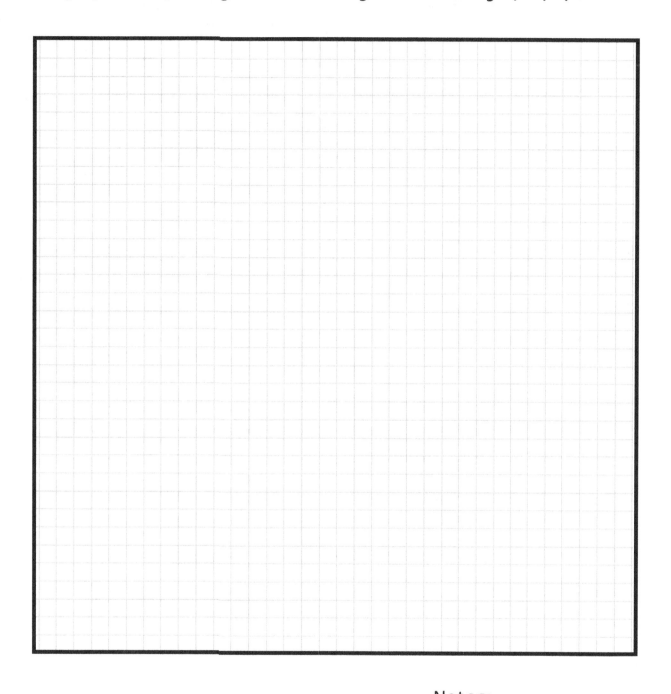

Notes:

_____

_____

_____

_____

Book of the Day

Choose a book from your stack that you want to focus on today.

Write and Draw to show what your are learning.

TITLE:_____

Travel Dreams Geography

Choose any City, any State or any Country:

Where would you like to go?

How far would you travel?

What would you pack?

----

what would you see?

What would you eat?

What is the weather like?

What makes this place unique?

Share an interesting fact:

Draw something you would see in this place:

Priority and Planning

Date:_____

A Quote

_____
_____
_____

To-Do List

_____
_____
_____
_____

My Plans

_____
_____
_____
_____

My Goals

_____
_____
_____

Notes:

_____
_____
_____
_____
_____

Object Lesson

Look at this picture.

List four things that you understand about the object.

1._____

2._____

3._____

4._____

Just be Creative.

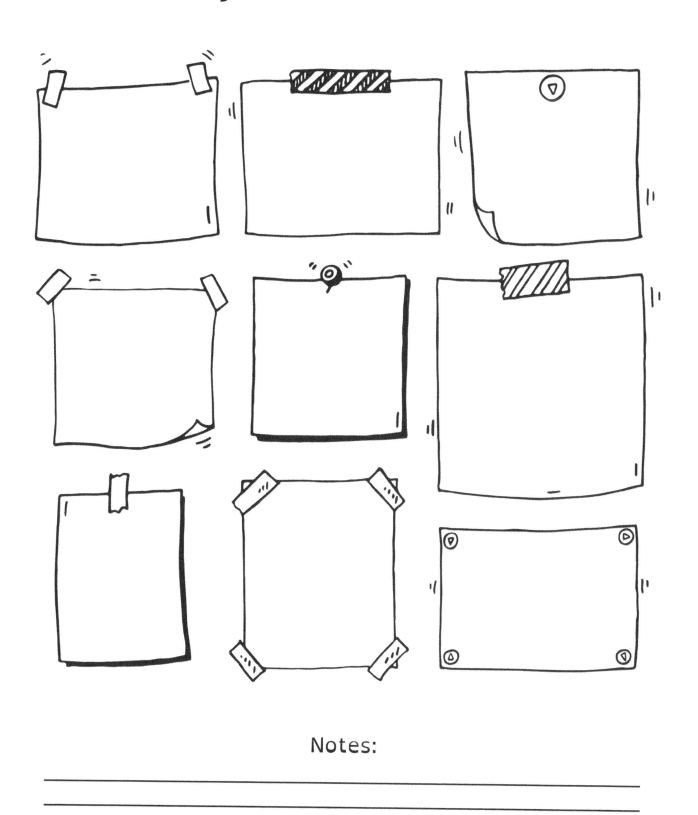

Notes:
_____
_____
_____

Nature Study

Go outside and make a realistic drawing of
something you find in nature.

Reading Time - 1 Hour (Set a timer)

Choose Four Books - Read from each book for 15 minutes.

Copy important words or pictures from each book here:

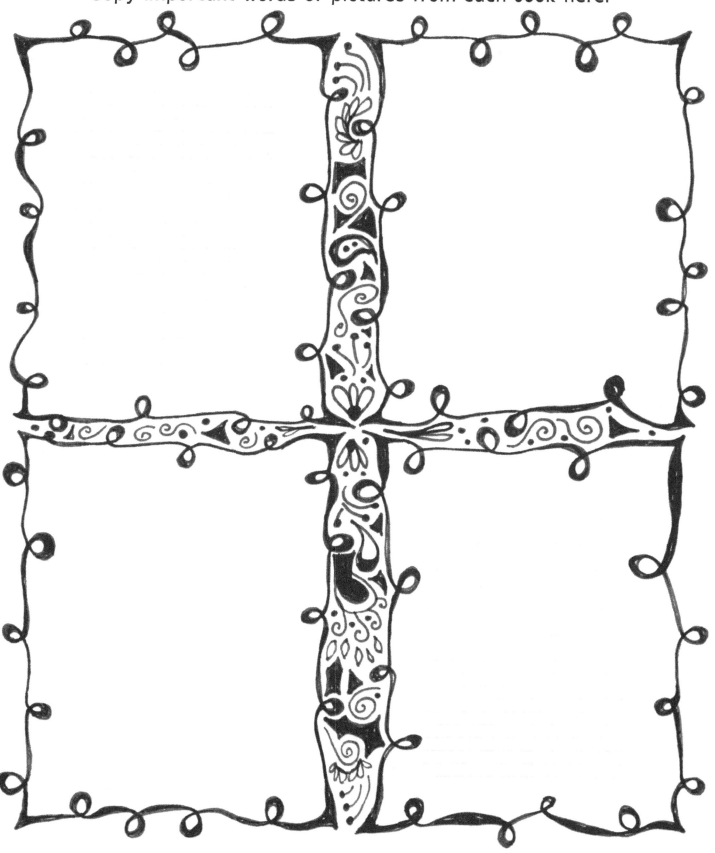

Spelling Time

Find 20 Words with 10 letters each.
Look around your house and in your
books for words. Write the words here:

_____   _____

_____   _____

_____   _____

_____   _____

_____   _____

_____   _____

_____   _____

_____   _____

_____   _____

Start Time:

Stop Time:

Screen Time!

Watch a Documentary, Educational Program, Movie, or Tutorial.

TITLE: _____

SUBJECT _____

LOCATION: _____

MESSAGE: _____

Rating:

AWFUL

BAD

LAME

YUCKY

OKAY

NICE

GOOD

GREAT

SUPER

Draw a Scene from the video:

Notes:

TITLE:

Use THIS PAGE for Math Practice

Or be creative and design something, like a house! You could make
graphs, maps or geometric designs with this graph paper.

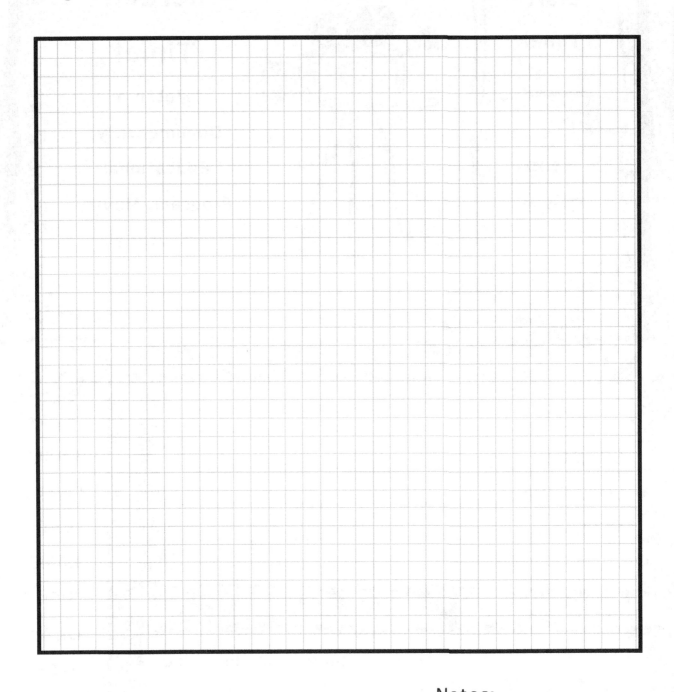

Notes:

_____

_____

_____

_____

Book of the Day

Choose a book from your stack that you want to focus on today.

Write and Draw to show what your are learning.

TITLE:_____

Font Writing Practice:

ABCDEFGHIJKLMNOPQRSTUVWXYZ

abcdefghijklmnopqrstuvwxyz

ABCDEFGHIJKLMNOPQRSTUVWXYZ

ABCDEFGHIJKLMNOPQRSTUVWXYZ

Abcdefghijklmnopqrstuvwxyz

Develop Your Own Style

Additional Books

Draw the covers of all the other books
that you use along with this journal.

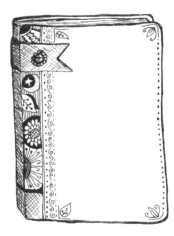
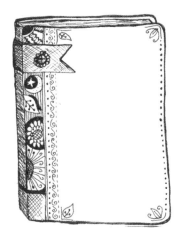
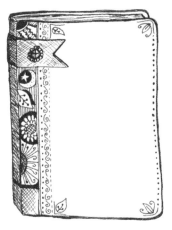

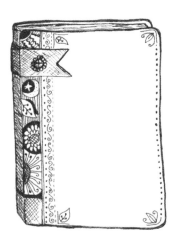

Additional Books

Draw the covers of all the other books
that you use along with this journal.

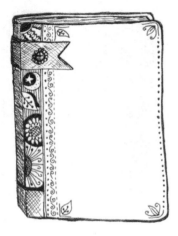
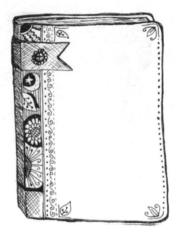
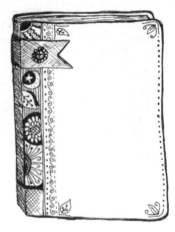

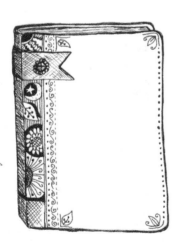

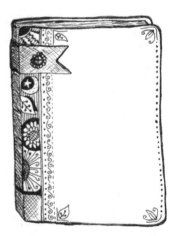

Additional Books

Draw the covers of all the other books that you use along with this journal.

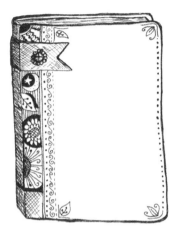
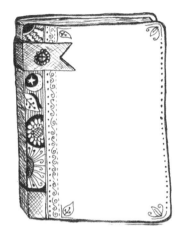

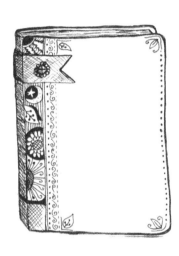
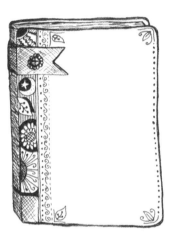

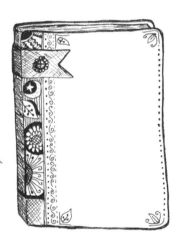

Additional Books

Draw the covers of all the other books
that you use along with this journal.

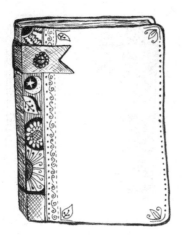

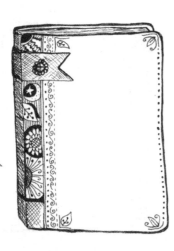

Additional Books

Draw the covers of all the other books that you use along with this journal.

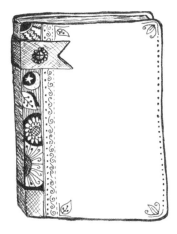

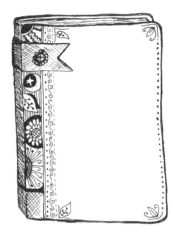

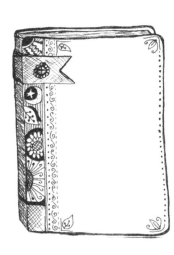

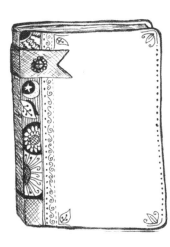

Additional Books

Draw the covers of all the other books that you use along with this journal.

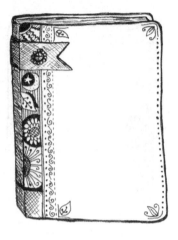 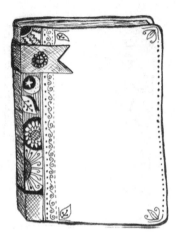 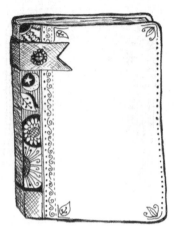

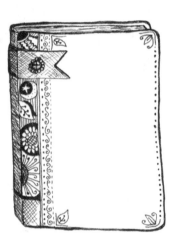 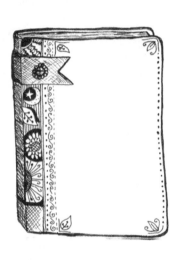 

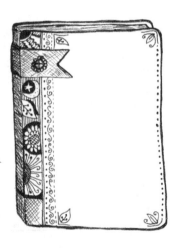  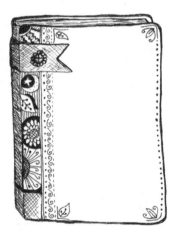

Brown Family Favorites for Homeschooling with Teens! 2016 List!

We enjoy learning with real books, rather than textbooks...

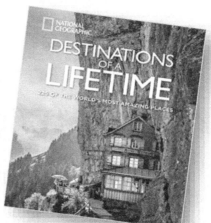

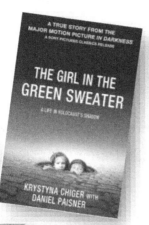

Do It Yourself
HOMESCHOOL
JOURNALS

Copyright Information

Contact Us:

The Thinking Tree LLC

617 N. Swope St. Greenfield, IN 46140. United States

317.622.8852 PHONE (Dial +1 outside of the USA) 267.712.7889 FAX

www.DyslexiaGames.com

jbrown@DyslexiaGames.com

Made in the USA
Middletown, DE
27 July 2024

58037027R00212